LOVELY
TRAGIC
MIRACLE

LOVELY
TRAGIC
MIRACLE

A Memoir
by
Karyl McKendry
with
Barbara Allen Burke

In Loving Memory of

Patrick Timothy McKendry

Dedicated to our children

Clancy Patrick McKendry
Sadie Kay Averill
Jesse Allen McKendry
Timothy James McKendry

I am so grateful for all of you.

—K. M.

Orchard

By Jon McKendry

The diligent Farmer lays an axe at the base.
We plead for His mercy.
Such a large, strong beautiful tree.
Surely it deserves more time.

For over the years it bore ripe,
Righteous, real fruit.
Does the Farmer know which tree
He is about to fall?

Surrounded by a forest of
Young, fruit-bearing saplings,
The orchard grows weary as
The final blow fells the giant.

The ground trembles, the crashing
Is heard throughout.
The awkward, awful silence is
Troublesome in the wake.

The roots that once tied the grove together
Dry in the naked sunlight.
The sun begins to beat down
Without the shade.

When it seems that all is lost,
The Farmer nurtures the young grove.
With the extra sun, water and care,
The saplings mature.

The roots that once connected the orchard
Are replaced by new growth.
As more giants rise in the absence,
Their branches reach out.

The trees grow accustomed to
The wind and the sun.
They begin to provide shelter
To other saplings.

The Farmer smiles as his orchard,
Once with one giant,
Now has many.
The process begins anew.

INTRODUCTION

I'm sitting in my chair at the dentist office where I work, leaning over the most beautiful three-year-old girl. She's so still and quiet, her sweet little mouth propped open with a rubber dam isolating her tiny teeth. I'm holding a suction, passing instruments back and forth to Dr. Strange in a simple, silent rhythm that comes from working together for over thirty years.

Whup-whup-whup-whup.

Suddenly, I am caught off-guard by the sound of a helicopter hovering somewhere just outside our building. Part of me—the logical, analytical part—knows that it is probably a trauma helicopter arriving at Lutheran Hospital next door to our offices. Still, the sound instantly transports another part of me, frightened and sick, to a place I have visited in my mind everyday for the past two years. Although I have never actually been there in person, I know the location by heart.

In this place, it is always just before dawn, pitch-black and cold. I'm standing at the edge of a deserted country road surrounded by the stubbled remains of wheat fields. The road, which for miles has run in a straight line, veers sharply at my feet, strewn with gravel and dirt. Up ahead, just off the curved pavement is my son Clancy's Ford pickup truck, tilting precariously on its top, windows smashed. A helicopter perches nearby, spotlights cutting through the pre-dawn darkness.

I run toward the truck in my mind, knowing what I will see but still hoping against hope that even now, after two years, I will be wrong. There, lying in the ditch, is my husband, Pat, still dressed in his camo hunting clothes. His chest is pinned beneath the upside-down cab of the truck, his eyes closed. Clancy, his face disfigured by fear, lies in the dirt next to Pat, his arm cradling his father's head.

I run to them and kneel on the frozen earth beside them. Every time I visit this place, I scramble to find something, anything, that I can do to make things turn out differently. I try to lift the heavy truck off of Pat. I try to bring the emergency vehicles closer, faster. I bend down and whisper in Pat's ear, willing him to hear me:

Hang on, Pat!

Just a little longer, honey.

They're on their way.

You're so strong. I know you can make it.

Just hang on!

Every day I whisper to him. Every day I wish for it to be changed. I breathe for Pat as the fire truck arrives. I watch Clancy help the fireman hook up the chain and lift the truck off Pat's chest. I imagine that with my help, we can save him. In my mind,

I yell for the EMT's to bring the AED machine.

At this point in my imaginings, the scene shifts from what I am told happened. I see a different outcome. Suddenly, I hear a heart rhythm beeping on the monitor. The rescuers from the Flight for Life helicopter rush over to Pat and stabilize him for the flight to Denver, maybe even landing at Lutheran's Hospital. Next I see Pat lying in a hospital bed, with me sitting beside him holding his hand.

I know this isn't what actually happened. I know the difference between the facts and a daydream. Still, I can't stop hoping for even a minor miracle, that my imaginings will come true.

They never do.

CHAPTER 1

BEGINNINGS

When I was born, my mother was afraid to name me. I'd arrived six-weeks prematurely by emergency caesarean, which was frightening enough back in 1966, and terrifying to my young parents, Bob and Bev Allen. To make matters worse, I'd made my appearance on the fifth anniversary of the death of my grandfather, my mother's dad. This wasn't a good sign, she decided. Her father had been both a hard-rock gold miner and part Choctaw Native American, and he was given to superstitions. Some of it had

rubbed off on my mom. She somehow couldn't shake the feeling that if she named me, I would die. My mother decided to pass on the job of naming me. Could she somehow foresee the shadow that would pass over me one day?

I had two older sisters—Barbara

and Karla, who were five and three—and my mother decided to ask them to pick my name. They thought "Carol" sounded pretty. My parents agreed, but changed the spelling to Karyl, which was how a high school friend had spelled it. Whatever the spelling, my name meant "song of joy." What did it mean to be born with both the shadow and the song?

With the exception of a brief period spent in Greenville, Texas, when I was a baby, I have lived in Colorado all my life. From as early as I can remember, we lived outside of town in a rural community named Hygiene. Yes, Hygiene. It got its name from Hygienic House, a sanatorium for tuberculosis patients sometime during the 1800's. We lived in a turn-of-the-century farmhouse at the end of a country lane. My best friend, Roger Brickman, lived in a farmhouse just down the road, and we spent lots of time outdoors, picking apples and grapes and strawberries, shelling peas on the porch, or feeding the pigs.

My parents completely remodeled our house, mostly by them-selves or with the help of nearby family and friends. We spent weeks in a house without a bathroom, running out to the barn in the middle of the night to use the make-shift outhouse. Barbara, Karla and I spent weekends holding pieces of lumber while my dad sawed the cuts, hammering up sheetrock, or picking up bent nails. I couldn't have known then how much of a foundation this would lay for my adult life, and for the lives of my own children.

We rode the bus into town for school. Once a week after school, my sisters and I would walk down the road from the schoolhouse, past the post office, and stop at Clark's general store where we purchased one piece of candy on credit. We then walked past the gas station and the diner to get to Hygiene Methodist Church where we had our weekly girl scout meetings, over which my mother, the scout leader, presided.

We belonged to a church that was in the larger town of Longmont, ten miles away. We spent most of every Sunday in town, going to Sunday school and the worship service in the morning. We were back in the evening for Youth Group and another service. I must have been about five or six years old when my Sunday school teacher, Mrs. Oppenhuizen, told us in five-year-old terms what it meant to become a Christian. She explained that it meant following the example of Jesus to become a source of help and hope in the world, taking a path of service and ministry.

These were pretty abstract concepts for a five year old. But even at such a young age, I knew that this was the direction my life should take. How did my little mind process the choice I was making? How could I know that this step would reverberate throughout my life, or that it would become so central to me four decades later when I faced the toughest challenge of my life? I'm sure I didn't completely understand. But Mrs. O's words made sense to me, and so my friend Roger and I both knelt on the floor in front of our chairs. Side by side, Roger and I prayed and asked God to forgive us from our sins and to save us. Thanks to this Sunday School teacher, I became a Christian. Mrs. O's funeral was the first I ever attended. They played a recording of her singing. It was weird to hear her voice after her death.

When I was eight years old, my parents, who had been foster parents, decided to adopt another child to round out our family. Her name was Karen, and she'd been removed from her family as a toddler because of abuse. Since then she'd been shuffled between several foster families, many of which had mistreated her as well. She was nine years old—a year older than I was—but was the size of a five-year-old. Because her school life had been so disrupted, my parents decided to have her stay back a year in school, so she and I were in the same grade. She became the fourth daughter, and my new roommate.

When Karen and I were in junior high school, my family moved to Wheat Ridge, a suburb of Denver, to be nearer to my dad's work.

What a transition! My gang of sisters was now reduced by one when Barbara went off to Oregon for college. Karla started her junior year at Wheat Ridge High School and Karen and I started 8th Grade at Manning Junior High School. We felt out of place in Wheat Ridge, which we quickly learned was an affluent part of town. While we had felt some of the differences before between the solidly middle class families like ours and those who had nicer clothes or took more vacations, Wheat Ridge felt like a different world.

The church we attended—Applewood Baptist Church—was also different. I'd literally grown up in our old church (the church nursery had my old crib and many of my toys), but I wasn't sure how to find a way to fit in with this new crowd and for the first few years just watched from the sidelines.

Fortunately, the church had excellent drama and music programs for kids. When I was 14, I decided to join a puppetry group that I thought would give me a chance to meet people my age.

There was one boy I especially wanted to meet. His name was Patrick McKendry. He was a year older, with sandy hair, great dimples, and the iciest blue eyes I had ever seen. He also went to another high school, so the only time I had a chance to see him was at church.

I wasn't sure if he noticed me or not. We talked during our puppet rehearsals, of course. And there was one time when he had just gotten his driver's license and he gave me a ride home from church in his mother's blue Cadillac. I sat next to him in the front seat of the car, too nervous to talk. When he pulled up to the curb in front of my house, I thanked him and went inside.

Then the puppet ministry was discontinued, and my connection was severed.

Still, I watched him from afar and learned a little more about  him. He was the youngest of five children. The oldest, Michelle, was the only girl in the family and, nine years older than Pat, was already married and gone. His brothers Russ, Steve and Dave all helped out with the family construction business.

Although Pat was active on his high school's golf team, he was also drawn to music. The following spring, we both joined the church youth choir when it started rehearsing a musical it would take on tour at the beginning of the summer. I don't remember the day when the acquaintance turned to a friendship, which then turned into a romance. I just know that during that musical, our relationship sparked. There were many rehearsals, and Pat and I spent all of that time together, getting to know each other. If there was a time when neither of us was involved in a scene, we spent it together. We took our lunch breaks together, and he drove me home every evening.

From that point on, we dated seriously. Still attending separate high schools, we got together on the weekends and evenings. During the summer, Pat worked in construction for his father and I filled my time with babysitting.

In the fall of my junior year in high school, I started working for Malcolm Strange, a pediatric dentist I met through our church. I went to Malcolm's office every day after school where I worked as an instrument technician. In the evenings Pat and I talked on the phone. Back then, the phone was a landline attached to the wall of the house, and I would stretch the long phone cord so I could lie on the floor of the hallway and talk. Of course, we continued to see each other at Wednesday night services at our church and most of the day on Sundays. During the week, Pat often visited an allergist whose office was next door to where I worked, and he would leave notes written on gum wrappers or scraps of paper under the windshield wiper of my car.

These two elements of my life—my growing love for this boy named Pat and my work for a dentist named Malcolm—became threads that would weave themselves through my transition into adulthood.

When we graduated from high school in 1984, Pat went to work full time with McKendry Homes, the construction business run by his brothers, Russ and Steve. The housing market in Denver had crashed during the mid-1980's, and the family felt it needed Pat, already a skilled builder, to help. Although all of his siblings had college degrees or professional training, college wasn't really in the cards at that time. Hindsight being twenty-twenty, this turned out to be his greatest regret.

I, on the other hand, had never considered college an option. I'd struggled in school for years, eventually being diagnosed with a learning disability. In addition to being dyslexic, I had trouble processing information visually. Although I could remember the lyrics to any song and recite memory verses better than anyone in my Sunday school class, I had trouble gathering information from reading. Since I expected that there would be a fair amount of reading required in college, I put the option out of my mind and told Malcolm I would like to continue working for him full time. He absolutely refused, wanting me to go to college instead. I worked full-time through the summer. Malcolm never mentioned it, but just let me think that at the end of the summer . . . well, I was done.

Finally, September rolled around and it was obvious that I was not in college classes. Only then did Malcolm relent and gave me full-time work. It ended up being a great education of its own. I was trained in almost every aspect of the pediatric dental business, and eventually ended up doing more restorative and surgical assisting.

My sister Karen had graduated from high school the same year as I did, but she struggled with her future. She got a job at a nearby daycare center. She was good with kids, soft-spoken and had a tender heart. However, her early history of neglect and abuse had apparently translated into an uncertain sense of herself. She drifted into friendships with people who were unemployed or drug users and developed a completely different circle of friends. She stopped showing up for work and eventually lost her job. One day, I came home from work and she was gone. She'd packed up and moved out without leaving any information. We would not see or hear from her for many years.

Our lives continued in this way for four more years—Pat and I both working and seeing each other as often as we could. I think people assumed we would eventually move past our high school romance. Pat was encouraged to try dating other people, but he was miserable during our separation and, after hearing a false rumor that I was seeing one of our mutual friends, he called and said he wanted to get back together.

My 21st birthday was in June of 1987. We celebrated with a family dinner at the McKendry house. My parents had been invited as well, along with all the other grown McKendry children. Pat's brother Dave had proposed to his girlfriend Michelle (called "Shell" to avoid confusion with the two other Michelles in the family) the night before, and this was both my birthday party and a celebration of Dave's engagement.

Years before, Pat's father Donny had purchased four diamonds, two matched sets, intending to give one to each son to be set in an engagement ring. Russ had used the first diamond when he married Tracy several years before. Steve had given the second diamond to his bride Shelly shortly after. Dave had just given away the third. One diamond remained.

We all sat in a big circle in his parents' huge family room. I opened all my gifts from other family members. Pat handed me my birthday present, a large wrapped box. I opened it to find clothes inside. In one corner of the box was a small crumpled bit of tissue paper. I unwrapped the crinkly paper and saw a sparkling, loose stone. It was a flawless .63 carat diamond that caught and reflected the light as I rolled it in my palm.

Pat's sister, Michelle, was the first to speak. "What does that mean?" she asked.

"She knows what it means," said Pat.

We started planning the wedding. Dave and Shell had already scheduled their wedding for October of that year. I didn't really want a winter wedding, and Pat, having waited so long, didn't want to wait a full year. The only day available at our church to have the wedding was September 25th, just three months away.

My mother did most of the wedding planning. She had owned a floral shop for several years and was both skilled and efficient. It came together quickly. That next week we all went to a bridal shop. I bought the first dress that I saw and picked the bridesmaids dresses that same evening with no hesitation.

The wedding was held at the church where we'd met. Our youth pastor officiated. We had pink and cream balloons, and a fabulous wedding cake. My mother did the flowers, and Malcolm videotaped the ceremony.

After the reception at a nearby Ramada Inn, we headed for our honeymoon at Pat's family's mountain house in Estes Park. Before leaving Denver, however, I saw an example of the meticulous attention to detail that would become a defining characteristic of my new husband. Our car, my Ford Bronco II, had been traditionally festooned in crepe paper and shaving cream, and Pat didn't want to leave anything on the car that could damage the paint. So we stopped at a car wash on our way out of town. We  later learned that all four of his siblings had stopped at the same car wash and got food at the Arby's next door after their own weddings. How completely freaky is that? There had been no talk of that before or after their weddings.

We stayed in Estes Park for only a few days. The summer tourist season was over and most of the shops and businesses had already shut for the winter. Instead, we just wanted to start our married life together. We'd dated long enough. Now we just simply wanted to live. We packed up our sparkling clean Bronco and headed for our new home, together.

Getting to Know
Clancy

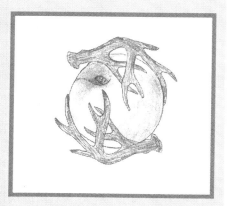

Pat and I had only been married about four months when we found out that our efforts to delay having children had failed. We were shocked but so excited at the same time. Once again God was showing us that His timing was not our timing. Pat, being the youngest of five children, wanted a big family of his own. We were not financially stable, but we were young and we didn't worry too much about it. On January 21, our precious baby boy was born. It was a difficult delivery, but our son was healthy and Pat was overjoyed.

Despite the encouragement from my boss to name the baby after him, Malcolm McKendry, we chose the name from our

favorite movie, *Man From Snowy River.* The man from this movie, named Clancy, was a rugged cattle herder from Australia. He was everything you'd want your son to be, strong and courageous but with the most gentle and quiet spirit. Clancy Patrick McKendry was the perfect Irish name for our 8 pound 3 ounce little boy. He lived up to the name early as he was drawn to horses, cowboy boots, chaps and cowboy hats. We took him to the rodeo every year and by age three he pretended to be riding bulls and roping cattle many hours of the day. He'd gallop around the house, swinging an imaginary lasso overhead, shouting, "out of chute number two, here comes Clancy McKendry."

My boss, Malcolm, really believed in teaching your children about working by having them involved in it with you, and he told me before Clancy was born that he wanted me to bring the baby to work with me. We had an unused room at the time and he helped me set it up as a nursery complete with a crib and changing table. We kept a bouncy seat and later a walker out in the treatment room itself for his awake times. I'm sure with OSHA and HIPPA and other regulations we wouldn't get away with that now, but this was the 80's. If I was busy with a patient and Clancy needed a feeding or a diaper change, one of my co-workers would gladly step in and help. This was the best of both worlds for me. I didn't have the heartache of leaving him, but still had the ability to earn money and be fulfilled at what I really enjoyed at work. He was an easy baby, but very active, so when he was about 9 months old he began to be too mobile for the office. My mom started watching him the three days a week that I worked.

Just two months shy of Clancy's second birthday, we had

Sadie. Although Clancy was still a toddler and required lots of attention, he didn't seem to mind sharing the spotlight with his baby sister. Clancy had a happy disposition and was easy to please.

He was also a little like a bull in a china shop! Early one Saturday morning, Pat and I were still sleeping when we heard an odd noise coming from the family room. I flew out of bed and rounded the corner to see Clancy on top of the fireplace hearth, balancing on his toes, his right arm stretched out to prevent our very large Jesus figurine from crashing to the ground. Jesus did lose his hand in that incident.

We decided that Clancy needed something to do. My mom still watched him and Sadie while I worked, but she had begun a new nursing career and was working the night shift at the hospital near us. She needed time to sleep. I enrolled Clancy and Sadie in preschool two mornings a week, and this worked out well for everyone. The preschool even offered an optional tap dancing class once a week. "Why not?" I thought to myself. So we put taps on Clancy's cowboy boots and signed him up. He is still, to this day, mad at me for that.

The Christmas before he turned four, we attended the preschool Christmas program. He had to wear white pants and a Christmas-y shirt for the tap dancing portion of the program. I couldn't find any white pants and resorted to buying white sweat pants. There he stood on the top row of the bleachers, taller that most of the other kids, sporting the bowl hair cut (he's still mad at me for that, too), white sweatpants and cowboy boot tap shoes. The class began to sing in their sweet little angelic voices, but when they reached the chorus it was Clancy's voice that rang out like a church bell on Sunday morning.

"Must be Santa, must be Santa, must be Santa, Santa Clause," he sang, his voice projecting over all the rest. The audience, filled with parents and grandparents, giggled every time the kids sang the chorus.

Clancy started elementary school the next fall. He was a good student and interacted well with the other kids. This was a good thing, because his brother Jesse was born when Clancy was six years old. And when brother James came along two years later in a sudden and surprising fashion, Clancy was protective and kind.

Throughout middle school and into high school, he never got into trouble and maintained a high GPA. His junior year in high school, he decided to play football. Yet he still loved to sing and had made the elite choir at his school, called Singers, which created a conflict. The Singers group had a mandatory retreat to kick off the year, which was the same time as the first pre-season football game. Clancy wanted to try to do both. He had to make a choice. He decided to go on the Singers retreat and therefore sat on the bench at the football games for quite a while. His love of  singing carried over onto the field and he was soon leading his team in the fight song at the end of every game. He'd often have the team singing together on the bus ride home from the away games.

One year, the school musical was *Oklahoma!* and Clancy landed the lead of Curly. The character was named for his curly hair and the director of the musical asked Clancy to perm his hair. After the musical we had to shave his head.

He entered college at Metro State University, still undecided about his career path. He was leaning towards a criminal justice degree but he was still interested in music. He wasn't required to declare a major, so he just did both. Even at the time, I was curious about how God would use Clancy and his assortment of talents and interests. I couldn't know that Clancy was about to face some of the most challenging times of his short life.

CHAPTER 2

A Tuesday in October

The month of October 2010 represented a new start for us. It had been a challenging year for us financially. Pat, who had for the better part of 25 years run a construction company with his brother Steve, had decided to set off on his own. The new company was called Tri-Mac, a business he could launch with his sons. Clancy took a break from college classes, excited to work full-time with his dad.

Although Pat looked forward to running his own shop, it couldn't have come at a more difficult time. The 2008 recession had crushed the building market in Denver and we knew that we would all have to scramble to make ends meet. I was working six days a week to provide a more regular income while Pat sought out different construction projects.

We decided to sell our home in Arvada, Colorado, a ranch-style house we had bought 15 years earlier and which Pat beautifully remodeled. It had been a great place to live. Pat's brother and sister-in-law, Russ and Tracy, and their kids lived just down the street, and for fifteen years we raised our children together in that neighborhood. We hosted regular gatherings for our church, L2, where Russ was the pastor. Pat had built the house to work the way we wanted it to, and the walls were imprinted with some of our family's best memories.

But it was time to move. We planned to use the equity to buy another house Pat could remodel and potentially sell for a profit. I wasn't especially worried. Being married to a builder, I had confidence that Pat would be able to create another wonderful home for our family wherever we landed.

We knew the housing market was terrible, and it took months to sell our house. Several offers fell through at the last minute. Finally, we had a buyer, signed the paperwork in July, and moved out. Unfortunately, we didn't have another house to move into. My parents live on a 40-acre property north of Denver and graciously invited us to move in with them. They had opened their home to our family many times in the past, and this was no different. Fortunately, the kids were out of school for the summer, but Pat and I continued to make the commute one-hour each way to work back in Denver. Clearly, we needed to find something before school started.

We felt that it would be best to remodel a house in an up-and-coming section of west Denver called the Highlands. We searched and searched, looking for something with a garage that could hold all of Pat's construction equipment and tools, and a house that could be expanded to hold our large family, plus our two miniature dachshunds, Lily and Dudley, and Skipper, the Maroon-bellied Conure parrot. Although Clancy had moved into his own apartment, Sadie, in college then, and Jesse, and James still lived at home.

We finally found what we were looking for on Wolff Street in the Highlands. It was a 1901 Victorian house with original brass hardware and sturdy oak floors. It sat on a large lot with a detached, three-car garage/shop that opened onto a back alley. A huge, old peach tree with  branches laden with ripe fruit stretched across a patio. Although the soft, red brick had been stuccoed a ghastly pink sometime in the '70's, the house had character and charm. What's more, Pat saw what he could do with the space to make it work for our family.

We closed on the house in September and couldn't wait to move in, even if it meant sharing the one, tiny bathroom and living in the house through all the stages of remodel. Pat and Clancy had taken on a few other construction jobs, but as soon as they finished, they planned to start demolition on parts of the house in hopes of getting a new addition framed in before the worst of winter hit. We had scrubbed the bathroom and kitchen appliances and removed the old linoleum from the kitchen floor. It didn't make sense to completely move in, so we stored most of our possessions at my parents' house. We spread mattresses on the floors, moved in a kitchen table and a small sofa, and unpacked just enough clothing and dishes to get by. We had lived in worse, and we were just happy to have landed in a place we could again call our home. We were all together: Pat, me, the kids, the dogs, and the bird.

Sunday, October 3rd, was one of those wonderful crisp, autumn days in Colorado, sunny and cool. After going to church

that morning, we all gathered back at our new house for lunch. Clancy came over to join us, and we all settled in the living room to watch football on the television we had propped on a table in front of the fireplace. It felt perfect. Later, I posted this message to Facebook:

Home is where your family is. We have always felt like that,
for we have lived with grandparents, in garages, and in homes

that should be condemned, and have been the happiest. October 3,
Sunday afternoon, in our home built in 1900 and in its original
state, the Pat McKendry family watched the Bronco game all
together in our normal fashion: Pat hollering, kids laughing, while
I read magazines. 'We are home,' I said.

Monday, October 4th, we were all back in our normal routines. Sadie took classes at Johnson & Wales, a college specializing in culinary arts. She wanted a career as a chef, and she and I dreamt about the possibility of the two of us opening a catering service or small coffee shop after she graduated in a couple of years. Sadie had just started a year of intensive training in different kinds of food preparation, and her courses started at 5:45 a.m. and continued until noon. Fortunately, her classes were only a fifteen-minute drive from our new house.

Jesse was a sophomore at Wheat Ridge High School, which was the school from which both Clancy and Sadie had graduated and, ironically, where I had gone to school. We'd decided to keep the kids in the same schools regardless of where we moved. Even though we were now in a new school district, Jesse and James's drive was still only about 5 minutes each way. Fortunately, Jesse had just earned his driver's license, which was both a relief for me as well as a source of worry. He loved driving, and he loved automobiles, especially the Ford trucks his dad always drove. He had spent hours in the garage with Pat and Clancy tinkering on cars, and was very competent. I knew he was a good driver. Unfortunately, so did he and I was afraid he wouldn't be as cautious as he should be. All my life, I'd had two basic fears. The first was that one of my kids would be accused of a crime that he or she didn't commit. The second was that one of my kids would get in a car accident that would severely injure or kill someone else. This was my third child to start driving.

James was in eighth grade at Manning Junior High School (which I had also attended). As the last of our McKendry children to have gone through the grades, almost every one of his teachers had had one of his siblings as a student before. James was finding his own way. He loved baseball and, what's more, was really good at it. He joined the Wheat Ridge Little League team, which was coached by Pat and another close family friend, Collin Myrick. James tolerated school and did just what he had to do to get through it, with the unending support and assistance of my mother, "Grammy." But baseball was where he was the most comfortable, and the area where he and his dad truly connected.

Pat was enjoying Tri-Mac. Even if his work for the day involved nothing more rigorous than paperwork at the desk in our home office, he would get up at 6 a.m., just as he always had, and put on his leather work boots and jeans. He was also studying to earn his contractor's license for the city of Denver so he could apply for the official building permit for the house. He would work all morning, and then at noon break for lunch. Every day after Sadie came home from school she would try out a new skill in making their lunch, a luxury of time together that they had never before enjoyed.

That Monday morning, Pat finished up the drawings to submit to the county. He and Clancy had an incentive to finish their work quickly because this would be a short week for them. They planned to take Wednesday off to go antelope hunting.

Pat and his brothers had grown up hunting with their

uncles. He and his brothers had started out hunting with guns for deer, elk and geese, and later switched to bow hunting. As our boys grew older, Pat invited them along. Although James would sometimes go goose hunting with Pat, it was usually Clancy and Jesse who clamored to go. There wasn't anything more exciting to them than getting ready for a hunting trip with their dad.

Pat had also started hunting with a couple of friends. Collin Myrick, James' baseball coach and the father of one of James' best friends, had joined Pat elk hunting a couple of years in a row. Another good friend of Pat's was Josh Bard, a professional baseball player he had met at church. We spent a lot of time with Josh, his wife Lindsey, and their kids. Pat had introduced Josh to hunting.

Josh had called Pat the previous week, reminding Pat that the antelope-hunting season ended on Wednesday, October 6th. "We've got to go," he said. Josh had a good friend with property out in eastern Colorado and he'd invited Pat to go there to hunt antelope. Pat agreed but asked if he could bring Clancy with him. This was one of the advantages of owning his own business that he had looked forward to. He could choose to take a day off and go hunting with his son.

Pat decided to tie the hunting trip in with business. Some of our good friends from church, Jeff and Jen, wanted to build a new patio at their house south of Denver, and asked Pat if he could manage the job, also hiring our friend Collin, who works as a stonemason. Jeff and Jen had invited all of us—me and Pat, Collin and his wife Dawn—to their house on Tuesday night so Pat and Collin could look at the property and then we could all have dinner.

Pat learned Jeff and Jen's house was on the way both to Josh and Lindsey's house, and to the hunting property where they would be driving the next day. We decided that Pat and I would drive out to dinner with Dawn and Collin. After dinner, Clancy would drive out in his truck, pick up Pat from Jeff and Jen's, and drive them both to Josh and Lindsey's house nearby. I would drive back to Denver with Dawn and Collin, and Pat and Clancy would spend the night at the Bard's house, giving them a shorter drive the next morning.

It was a great evening. After Pat and Collin took the measurements, we had dinner sitting around the table, eating pizza and talking. I decided to ask a question. What items, if any, did everyone have on their bucket lists? We went around the table. I now can't remember what the others were. I remember saying that I really wanted to go to Europe.

Pat went last. "I want to walk my daughter down the aisle," he said, "and I want to hold a grandbaby." That was it. That was all he wanted.

Dinner was over and everyone started getting their coats and saying goodbye. I was tired and didn't feel up to driving, so Collin said he would drive my car. Pat walked out to the car with me, and came around to the passenger side door to say goodbye. He leaned down and kissed me.

"Don't worry about me," I said. "I'll just be working tomorrow."

"Whoa," said Collin, a little surprised by my sarcastic tone.

I climbed into the car. "Don't worry, I'm just kidding. Pat knows how thrilled I am that he gets to do this."

I waved at Pat as we drove away.

CHAPTER 3
OCTOBER 6, 2010

It took a while for me to piece together what happened the next morning, but for many months I could picture it as clearly as if I were there.

Pat's alarm went off at 2:15 a.m. Normally a wakeup call this early would seem insane, but for Pat, Clancy and Josh, looking forward to a day hunting antelope, it was just a part of the adventure. They'd woken in darkness, dressed in their camo gear, and loaded Clancy's truck. They were only planning a day trip, so they traveled light. Pat and Clancy had each brought a small bag for the overnight stay at Josh's house, and they threw these bags in the small back seat of Clancy's navy blue pick-up truck. The rest of the gear went in the bed of the truck. Josh kissed a sleeping Lindsey goodbye and the three men climbed in the truck for the long drive. It was Clancy's truck, so he took the driver's seat. Pat decided that Josh should have the passenger seat, and he hopped in the smaller back seat with their extra luggage, twisting sideways so he, himself over six feet tall, would fit. I imagine them in that car, laughing and loud in the early dark. There really was little else that Pat—or Clancy—enjoyed as much as this.

By 3:45 a.m., they were nearing Hugo, Colorado, and stopped at a roadside gas station to get fuel for the truck and food for themselves. Josh insisted on paying for the gas so he got out to man the pump. Clancy and Pat picked up cold sandwiches, drinks and snacks they could eat later in the day. They also grabbed large cinnamon rolls wrapped in cellophane and cups of bad coffee for breakfast. They got back in the truck and headed out. Clancy decided he couldn't juggle the cinnamon roll while driving, so he set it aside. His dad and Josh told him not to worry; they were the World's Worst Cinnamon Rolls. Josh again rode shotgun, preparing to act as navigator to his friend's hunting property and Pat, balancing a cup of coffee in one hand, positioned himself in the middle of the back seat. For some reason—perhaps because he thought they were almost at their destination, perhaps he felt cramped in the back seat, or maybe because his hands were full— Pat didn't fasten his seatbelt.

They took off down Highway 71, south of Limon, and drove for another thirty minutes. The cab of the truck was warm against the cold of the rural countryside. Eventually, Josh instructed Clancy to turn left onto Highway T, a two-lane, chip-sealed road heading east. It was quiet and dark, especially away from freeway lights or towns. Clancy could see only the small stretch of road illuminated by his headlights.

The road was in bad shape. There was so much dirt and dust

on the pavement it made a sort of yellow glare in his headlights. There were no lines on the pavement, even to mark the shoulders, and it was hard to distinguish where the pavement joined the graveled edges of the road. Clancy slowed his speed..

"I think we have a straight road for a while," said Josh. "You could pick it up a little."

Clancy didn't feel comfortable going any faster. He stole a glance at his speedometer. He was going exactly 45 miles per hour. He couldn't see a speed limit sign (which we later learned was 55 mph) but he felt comfortable at the lower speed, a decision that would end up providing a lot of comfort in the coming days and months. He concentrated on seeing the road unfold in front of him, which rolled up and over a gentle hill in one, long straight line. It was now nearing 4:30 a.m., still an hour and a half before sunrise. He only had to drive straight on County Rd. T for a little longer. They were almost there. I can almost feel the excitement building in the cab of that truck.

Suddenly, the road in front of them seemed to stop. Although Clancy intended to keep driving straight ahead, the road unexpectedly banked sharply to the right. What he didn't know, couldn't know, was that he had come to an intersection where County Road T crossed County Road 23. The chip-sealed paving of County Road T, on which he was driving, ended abruptly and turned to grey gravel. The pavement, on the other hand, swerved to the right onto a sweeping bypass of the intersection, connecting Highway T with Highway 23. The roadway was banked on its outer edge, like an Indy car course, casting everything beyond it into shadow. Just beyond the intersection was a farmhouse, sheltered by some of the only trees around for miles. To Clancy, driving 45 miles per hour with only his headlights to guide him, it appeared that the road in front of him disappeared, and that if he continued straight ahead, he would plow into the farmhouse and the trees. In that fraction of a second, he felt he had no choice but to try to make the corner. He stomped on his brakes to reduce his speed and cranked the steering wheel hard to the right.

Physics were against him. Clancy tried to steer the heavy truck around the corner, but just when the back tires would

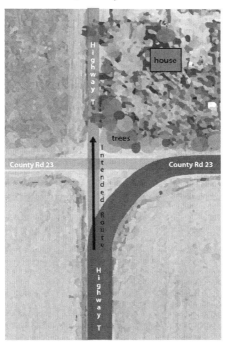

have gripped to give him traction, the centrifugal force pushed the driver's side tires off the banked edge of the road, landing in loose, powdery dirt. The truck kept sliding, and the force tipped the truck onto the driver's side. Metal hit dirt, and glass exploded when the back cab window and one of the back side windows blew out. The truck continued to roll onto its top, compressing the roof of the cab. Clancy heard the eerie sound of crunching metal, the shattering pop of breaking glass. The truck would probably have continued to roll and slide had the bed of the truck not rammed against one of the large trees in front of the farmhouse at the edge of the road.

Although the accident took place in a matter of seconds, Clancy felt that time slowed down. It was a strange combination of being strapped in, but feeling airborne, in free fall. Once rolling, he couldn't manipulate the truck and became a rag doll along for the ride.

Finally, the gut-wrenching rolling stopped. Utter silence replaced the crash and clatter of the accident. Clancy and Josh found themselves dangling upside down in the front seat in the dark, held up by their seat belts.

Clancy's first thought was that he was fine. Because he had survived the crash relatively untouched, it didn't occur to him that there could be any serious injury. He didn't even know to worry. His mind immediately jumped to the fact that his truck was probably totaled and their day of hunting had come to a stunning end. They'd have to figure out how to get the truck towed, and find rides back to Denver.

He heard Josh calling out, "Is everybody okay?

No answer. Sitting in the dark, this didn't surprise Clancy. The men in his family, his father included, typically responded to troubles or irritations by getting quiet for a few moments. Clancy himself didn't answer right away, and wasn't surprised that his dad said nothing.

"Is everybody okay?" Josh asked again.

"I'm okay," Clancy answered. Yet there was still no answer from his dad, which was strange. For the first time he felt worry. And fear. A tight knot formed in the pit of his stomach.

Clancy unbuckled his seatbelt and fell to the roof of the upside-down truck. It wasn't much of a fall because the cab had been compressed, and he found himself on his hands and knees on the roof of the cab. He crawled out of his broken window. He looked back and saw for the first time that his dad wasn't in the truck.

Josh, still suspended by his seatbelt, was stuck. Clancy, worried that the truck could be leaking fuel, stopped to help Josh get out of his seat belt and out of the truck before the two of them started looking around for Pat.

"Dad! Where are you? Dad, answer me!"

"Pat! You okay?"

No answer. They figured he must be unconscious. They scrambled around the wreckage, their eyes slowly adjusting to the darkness. They had walked away from the truck, but as they returned, heading back toward the front of the wreckage, they found him. The truck had landed top down at the bottom of an incline that angled down from the roadbed. In the rollover, Pat had somehow been thrown through the smashed window and landed underneath the passenger side of the cab. He laid in the bottom of a shallow ditch, the full weight of the truck pinning just a small section of his chest to the ground.

They ran over to him. He was barely breathing, struggling to take each breath into crushed lungs. Other than the corner of the cab that pinned the left side of his chest, the rest of Pat's body was exposed. The passenger door of the cab had opened and pushed his arm back over his head. Clancy tried to shut the door to free his arm, and instead kicked the door open wider to give Pat some room to rest his arm by his side.

Josh and Clancy scrambled to free him. Both strong men, they tried to shift the truck, but it had rolled down an incline, and lifting it off Pat meant trying to roll it back uphill. They tried to dig out the dirt beneath him, but it was frozen and compacted. Josh got on his cell phone and tried calling 911, but couldn't get service, so Clancy found his cell phone to call. He looked at the time. It was 4:30 a.m. He called 911, only to be frustrated again when he and Josh couldn't figure out how to give directions to the paramedics who would be coming from the nearest town of Limon, some 30 or 40 minutes away.

Fortunately, the farmer who lived in the nearby house had heard the squeal of tires and the crash and knew what had happened. It wasn't the first accident he had seen at the site, and he came out to investigate. He was able to give directions to the paramedics. Help was on the way. Emergency dispatch was sending out firetrucks, an ambulance, and a Life Flight helicopter.

Clancy laid down in the dirt, stretching his long body out on the right side of his father. He put his phone on speaker and set it on the ground next to Pat's head so he could talk to paramedics and have his hands free. Pat's head was tipped back at an awkward angle, making it difficult to breathe. Clancy put his left arm underneath Pat's neck to support his head, and held Pat's right hand with his own.

"Hang in there, Dad," he said. "Help is on the way. You just have to keep breathing."

Clancy started praying. He prayed the Lord's Prayer out loud, hoping Pat could hear the words. He prayed for help, for strength, for guidance. He told his dad that he loved him. Finally, he kissed Pat's forehead, something he had never done before. Pat normally shaved his hair to the scalp, so Clancy was surprised by the short, prickly feeling of the hair on his head.

Every thirty seconds or so, Pat would take a tortured breath. Clancy kept talking, his eyes watching the western horizon for the lights of an ambulance or a fire truck. He prayed for them to hurry, to get there while his father's irregular breaths kept coming.

The sun was starting to come up. The sky lightened enough that Josh and Clancy could see the dark, flat farmland take shape beneath a pink sky. It took thirty long minutes for the emergency vehicles to appear over the edge of the horizon. They were still a mile or so away, but they were coming.

"Just hang on, Dad," Clancy pleaded. "They're almost here!"

Pat took one more shallow breath, and let it out. And then he was still, his head heavy on Clancy's arm. He was gone. It was 5:15 a.m.

The paramedics scrambled from the ambulance when they arrived, assessing the situation. There were no vital signs, but they were limited in what they could do until they moved the truck. A fire engine pulled up and Clancy ran and asked them for a chain to hoist his truck. He grabbed one end of the chain and stretched it over the top of his pickup and hooked it to the cab so that when the fire engine pulled, it would roll the truck up off of Pat's body and not across it. As soon as the truck lifted, Clancy grabbed both of Pat's hands and pulled him free. He took a pair of scissors from the paramedic and cut off Pat's shirt. Instantly, the EMT's and paramedics swarmed Pat and tried to resuscitate him. Clancy stayed with his father, working the bag mask while an EMT did chest compressions. Somehow, they got Pat onto a back board and continued to work. Finally, a state trooper came and pulled Clancy from the scene in order to question him. Reluctantly, Clancy left Pat's side and went with the policeman.

Clancy sat in the back of the squad car, trying to fill out an accident report. By this time, the sun was fully risen, and the scene looked completely different from when the accident happened. How different it had all seemed in the dark. Clancy noticed a Life Flight helicopter thunder across the fields, hover over the accident scene, then land on the road. The Life Flight technicians jumped to the ground, but no one seemed to be moving his dad to the helicopter. They weren't rushing him to the hospital. Finally, a paramedic came and found Clancy.

"I'm sorry," he said, "but your dad didn't make it."

Clancy went to the back of the ambulance where they had placed his dad's body and just sat there looking down at him. Josh climbed in the back with him and they sat there together, saying goodbye.

Eventually, they climbed down from the ambulance. After that, the medics checked out Josh and Clancy, who were rattled and banged up. Clancy said he was fine, but when Josh mentioned that his neck hurt, they decided to take both of them to the town of Hugo, a 45 minute drive away, to be checked out at the hospital.

Clancy and Josh prepared to get into a different ambulance for the ride to Hugo. Before stepping into the back, Josh waited. He decided he needed to make a phone call.

CHAPTER 4

OCTOBER 6, 2010:
7:30 A.M.

M y own alarm went off at 6:15 a.m. that Wednesday morning. It was cool in the house when I got up, so I threw on a sweatshirt before going downstairs. Sadie was asleep on the couch. She was supposed to be at school early that day, but felt the flu coming on the night before. She'd emailed the chef who was her teacher to say she wouldn't be coming in. Jesse left for school at 6:45 a.m., and James and I were leaving soon. I've had back problems for years which are mediated by a weekly massage, and I had an appointment first thing that morning with Cindy Betz, a friend and massage therapist. I would first drop James at school, go to my appointment and then to work. I checked on Sadie, but she was still asleep, so at around 7:00 a.m. I called to James and the two of us walked out to the garage at the rear of our property where my car was parked.

Backing out of the garage into the alley was a tricky maneuver, and I was concentrating when my cell phone rang. It was Josh. Weird. I couldn't imagine why he would be calling when they were off hunting. I let it ring until I got the car out, and started down the alley. I answered the phone.

"Karyl, this is Josh," he said. "Are you sitting down?"

"I'm driving James to school?" I said. "Why?"

Josh paused for a second, then said, "There's been a terrible accident."

I stopped the car and put it in park. My first thought was that something had happened with the guns. Someone had been shot by accident.

"Are you sitting down?" Josh asked again. I told him I was. "There's been a rollover."

I don't remember the next few moments. Somehow I got the car back into the garage. Somehow I ended up standing in our back yard next to James. Josh gave me the basic details. They'd been driving near Hugo, just minutes away from their destination when the road curved unexpectedly and they'd had to take a sharp corner. The truck rolled over. Pat was thrown and somehow pinned underneath the truck.

"We tried and tried, Karyl." Josh was crying. "But Pat didn't make it."

My husband was dead, and yet I couldn't seem to get my brain to acknowledge that fact. I just couldn't believe that it was true. Instead, my focus shifted to Josh, and that he had to be okay. I felt responsible for his family.

47

"Are you okay?"

He told me he was fine. A little banged up. They were taking him to the hospital to check him out. Clancy declined any medical attention and after saying his goodbyes to Pat, decided he would go with Josh.

I still had my phone in my hand with Josh on the line. James and I started to go back into the house, but the door was locked and I couldn't seem to unlock it. I handed my keys to James, screaming for him to open it. He unlocked the door and followed me into the kitchen.

I walked into the house holding my head in my left hand with my phone in my right hand, yelling for Sadie.

She sat up from her place on the couch. She thought I must have hit my head with the garage door.

"What?" she asked.

"Daddy was killed in a car accident."

She didn't really understand what I said at first as I forced the air out of my lungs to speak. I said it again, and this time she was able to understand, even though my panicked, breathless mutterings barely sounded like words.

"Oh **no**!" Sadie screamed. She began to whimper with her head in her hands rocking back and forth. Our home phone started to ring. At some point when I was standing in the yard, I had just quit talking to Josh on my cell phone, so he called me back on our home phone. Sadie was running around crying hysterically while James and I were collapsed on the couch sobbing. The phone kept ringing. Finally, Sadie picked up the phone and muttered a hello. Josh, familiar with her voice since she had lived with them as their nanny for three summers, was caught off guard, expecting to talk to me again.

"Oh Sade, I'm so sorry" he said. Then Josh put Clancy on the phone and Sadie and I both talked to him. He said he was going to the hospital with Josh and would need someone to come and pick him up. I told him to call me when he got to the hospital.

I needed to have people around me. I called Tracy on her phone. She picked up.

"Trace?"

"What?"

"Pat is dead, Pat is dead."

Tracy fell to the floor in shock. Russ was sitting in his office and could hear me crying out over the speaker. Tracy repeated the news to Russ. Russ stood there for a moment not saying anything. It felt surreal. Tracy, finding it hard to believe the news, returned to our phone call.

"Do you want me to come over?" she asked.

"Yes" I bellowed.

I ended the call with Tracy, and then started dialing my parents' number. My mom picked up the phone and I told her the news. She told me later that the blood instantly drained from her face and my dad knew by looking at her that something was terribly wrong. I could imagine them in the kitchen, listening to my words, already gathering coats and keys and wallets for the drive south to Denver. I was so upset that they didn't even really understand if Clancy was ok or injured. After they left their house to drive down, they called me again to ask if Clancy was ok.

My mind was spinning. I have never, before or since, so understood the concept of time standing still. In the half hour before Russ and Tracy arrived, I felt that time stopped. While waiting for my parents to arrive in Denver, time just would not pass. I felt suspended, trapped. Lost.

I somehow had the capacity to remember that Cindy was expecting me for a massage for which I obviously would not come. I couldn't handle another phone call, so I sent her a text message: "Cindy, there's been an accident. Pat's with Jesus."

Sadie was in as much shock as I was, but she seemed compelled to action. She phoned my sister Barbara in Oregon to let her know, and asked her to call our sister Karla. She called some of our other friends. She wanted her brothers around her and said she was going to Jesse's school to pick him up. She wanted to get in the car and drive to Hugo to get Clancy. She seemed panicky to me, and the last thing I wanted was to have her on the road. I told her we would have Dawn Myrick call the school and tell Jesse that someone was coming to get him.

Russ and Tracy arrived first. I ran out of the house and into Russ's arms and then to Tracy's. We just stood there, embracing each other on the sidewalk for a long while.

I felt that I needed to stay at the house so that anyone could reach me if they needed to. I felt I needed to stay put. I wasn't sure where they, whoever they were, would take Pat's body. Would they need me to identify him or would they allow me to see him? I needed to find some stable place to stand. I felt a strong need to hold Pat's Bible and carried it around with me. That book stayed close to me for the next several days. His morning quiet time, time learning scripture and talking to God, was the center of his being.

Holding his Bible made me feel connected to him in the way that mattered most.

Someone needed to go get Jesse so I asked Russ to pick him up. Collin Myrick drove Russ in his Jeep to the school. Jesse told us later that he was sitting in his math class when someone came in and handed him a written message asking him to come to the office. That moment stays vivid in his memory, walking down the halls of the high school, flipping the red slip of paper over and over in his fingers, wondering what was going on but having no idea that his life was about to be irreversibly altered. He walked into the office. He didn't see anyone for a few minutes, then all of a sudden, Russ appeared behind him. His first reaction was that Russ was there to tell him something had happened to Tracy. Instead, he heard that his father, whom he had just seen the day before, was gone.

Jesse began walking to the back lot where his truck was parked. Russ suggested that Collin drive him to his truck. Jesse declined. Russ offered to drive and Jesse said no. He had backed into a pretty tight spot upon arriving that morning, and it would be tough to pull out. Russ told him, "You can drive that thing better than me anyway. You're just like your dad. You could park that thing on a sticky note."

That truck was Pat's baby. He had kept it in immaculate condition for many years. It was work to maintain all the components that kept the more than five hundred horsepower engine running. Pat and I had just decided that Jesse could buy the truck from us and drive it. Pat would look for a truck more suitable for towing trailers and hauling materials needed for work. That charcoal blue metallic King Ranch F-150 would become, for Jesse, what Pat's Bible was to me—a way to stay connected to his dad. Collin led the way home, with Jesse and Russ following them. I heard the rumble of all that horsepower approaching, and went to the garage to meet Jesse. He backed that beautiful truck perfectly into its very tight spot. How could he manage that task with such distraction? I remember being amazed even in that moment of extreme grief and disbelief. He stepped out and all I could do was stand there and hug him.

My parents arrived from Berthoud, and we decided that they were the best ones to go pick up Clancy. All the kids wanted to go—they seemed drawn to just be together in the same place—so they all piled into my parents Mazda for the drive to Hugo. Before they left, Sadie came to hug me goodbye and placed a chain around my neck. It was a thick chain that normally held a pendant I often wore when I worked in the church nursery. It was heavy and big and babies loved to look at it. This morning, however, Sadie had replaced the pendant with Pat's wedding ring. Pat had a "working" wedding ring he wore to work and on his hunting trip. This was his "dress" wedding ring, saved for special occasions that I now wore on a chain around my neck.

Everyone started showing up. Carol Kistner, one of my oldest friends who had worked with me since the beginning at the dental office, was one of the first. She showed up with one of her children and just sat quietly nearby. Co-workers from my office came, taking shifts so that everyone had an opportunity to come. One of the dentists, Courtney, came into the office on her day off to take patients so that another dentist, David Strange, Malcolm's son and a friend of mine since high school, could come. Pat's parents Don and Joan showed up, and Pat's other siblings. Wave after wave of friends kept arriving, gathering around our limited furniture and spilling into the front yard. Another friend, Rich Wyatt, brought over folding chairs so that people would have a place to sit.

Finally, my parents arrived with Clancy and the kids. I ran out to meet Clancy in the front yard, and he bolted from the car and ran to me with his arms stretched open wide, like a small child who was lost in a grocery store. He was still wearing his camo gear and his face was streaked with blood. He was so tall, but reached down to hug me, sobbing. "I'm sorry, I'm sorry, I'm sorry," he said, over and over. I went to wipe the blood off of his face and he grabbed my hand to stop me. "No, it's Dad's," he said.

I reached up and grabbed his face with both of my hands and made him look me in the eyes. I said the words for the first time that I would repeatedly say to him over the next many months.

"Honey, this isn't your fault. You didn't even know about this trip and you didn't plan it. Your dad put it all together. Your dad asked you to take your truck, and he made you drive. It's not your fault. You believe that God is sovereign, right?" He nodded. "This was your dad's appointed time. It's not your fault."

We stood together like that for five full minutes, with me trying to get this message across to him. He finally seemed to know and understand that I didn't blame him. That we didn't blame him. All of his cousins circled around to embrace him, and no one would leave him alone. He wouldn't wash the blood from his face, and he wouldn't change out of his clothes.

Toward the end of the day, I looked up to see Jim Teasdale

standing in the doorway. Jim was a friend who worked as a missionary in Africa. He had been in North Carolina when he heard the news and caught the first flight out he could find. Pat, Clancy, Sadie and I had spent five weeks in Kenya with Jim along with Russ, Tracy and two of their kids. This trip was one of the highlights of Pat's life. Everyone assumed after we were in Kenya that Pat and I would end up ministering there as well. It seemed the perfect fit for Pat. The only problem was that it didn't fit me at all. I have an irrational fear of snakes and germs. I was adamant that we were not moving to Loiyangalani, Kenya. When I saw Jim standing there in the doorway of my house in Denver, however, I felt like my selfishness had cost me dearly. If I could have Pat back I'd be willing to go, snakes and all.

I had all of my kids around me, many of the members of my family, and most of my friends. Still, I felt lost. I didn't know how I would get through the next five minutes, let alone the next hour, day, week or year. I couldn't think that far ahead. I could only take one breath at a time. It seemed as if every breath was intentional and difficult.

None of us felt that we could sleep in the house on Wolff Street. What had just the day before felt like an exciting project, a house filled with hope and a great future, now just felt like a dilapidated, broken structure. I kept asking aloud that day, "God, how could you take Pat away and leave me with this house in this state?" We all decided that we would go over to Clancy's apartment to sleep. We got ready to load up in the cars to head over, when I felt that I needed to have Tracy near me.

I knew that Tracy and Russ were having nearly as hard a time as I was. Pat was Russ's brother. Together, they were probably our closest friends. They were in real pain and probably needed each other's company and the support of many other people to get through. Even knowing all that, I knew I needed Tracy with me to get through the night, and she agreed to come. Fortunately, Jim Teasdale was there and said he would go home with Russ.

We arrived at Clancy's little apartment and crashed on an assortment of beds and hide-a-beds, I laid down next to Tracy, but couldn't sleep. I stared at the ceiling, crying, my mind filled with images of Pat lying on the gravel road under the truck. I imagined speaking our last words to each other. Tracy slept from time to time, and she would wake up frequently to hug me and try to comfort me. I got up several times in the night to make sure the kids were okay. Clancy slept hard.

Eventually, the dark grew lighter and the next day came. I laid in a strange bed with my sister-in-law beside me and was hit with the reality that this would be the first day of my life without Pat.

CHAPTER 5
FIRST DAYS

When Tracy woke up, we got out of bed. Sadie was awake as well. We all felt like we could use some coffee so the three of us pulled on shoes and coats over the t-shirts and sweats we'd slept in and drove to the Starbucks Coffee near Clancy's apartment. We'd left the boys asleep in the apartment. I felt that whatever few minutes of absence from Pat's death they could get was a blessing for them, and I couldn't bear waking them.

The Starbucks had just three or four customers at that time of the day, but I wasn't sure I could manage the small task of walking up to the counter and ordering a drink. Standing in the coffee shop where everyone's lives went on just as it had the day before was agony for me. I saw a stack of newspapers for sale and read the date on the masthead: Thursday, October 7, 2010. The world had gone on. The new day had come. For most people, this was unremarkable. For me, it was heart-wrenching. I thought, not for the first or last time that day or the days that followed, that I would prefer just not to move on with the rest of the world. I just didn't want to face a day, the first of the rest of my days, in which Pat wouldn't be alive.

We got our coffee and decided to head back to the Wolff house where we knew people would soon be gathering. Tracy called her daughter Elizabeth and asked her to bring over a change of clothes and a toothbrush. The boys were still sleeping so we left a note, asking them to call us so we could send someone to get them when they were ready.

The house was cold. The furnace had been acting up since we'd moved in. It was a problem Pat had been planning to fix. The smell of old food permeated the little air making it to my lungs. There was still a pot of stew on the stove from the day before, cold, with thick, congealed skin on the surface. Chairs and cheese trays were scattered everywhere. My parents arrived and we all spent the next half hour just picking up.

I started by picking up folding chairs and tripped over something. I looked down and saw Pat's Sanuk shoes. The day before, with all the craziness and commotion of people coming and going around the house, his loafers had stayed just where he had left them. It was one of those little things, those sudden punches to the gut that sent me over the edge. I stood there and just sobbed. My parents saw me and rushed over to comfort me. I knew they wanted to help. I knew they wanted to make me feel better. But there was nothing that would make me feel better. All I wanted was for Pat to be standing there in his shoes.

Flowers started arriving. Vase after basket after pot of flowers came through the front door of our falling-down, torn-up little house. We didn't have a lot of furniture on which to display them, so we set them on windowsills, on the railings of the front porch, on the kitchen counters. The flowers brought to mind how the sender had known Pat, and these were welcomed thoughts. They provided a good distraction from the ugliness of the house we were all gathered in. When we filled the downstairs rooms, we started carrying flower arrangements upstairs to the bedroom.

Pat and I had been sleeping on a queen-sized mattress placed in an anteroom just off the staircase. It had no door, and the mattress took up most of the floor space. We had a little wooden table beside the bed. As I placed a bouquet on the table I saw the book that Pat had been reading, his place marked by a flat-sided construction pencil. An empty beer bottle sat on the unfinished wood floor next to a pair of his work boots, lined up precisely. I sat on the bed, undone again, wishing I could leave the book, the bottle and the boots exactly as they were forever. These were some of the last things he had touched. I touched them, wishing I could feel his hands again.

People showed up at the house again for the second day, scattered through the kitchen, spilling into every room, spreading out through the yard. Josh and Lindsey came over in the afternoon. I was already in the front yard when they arrived. Josh hugged me and we both cried. Lindsey told me that he'd been having a hard time. He didn't really want to talk about what had happened. I'm sure he was dealing with his own grief and anguish. I couldn't imagine how hard it must have been to come to the house and participate in the grief of my family and me. But I was glad to see him and to hug one of the last people to see Pat. I felt such gratitude to him for being the one to tell me about the accident, sparing Clancy from having to make the call.

Josh took both of my hands in his and said, "I'll tell you anything you want to know."

I knew what I wanted to hear. "I need to know that someone told Pat that they loved him." I'm not sure if he even said yes to that question, but he wanted me to be assured that he would go to his grave telling anyone and everyone that this wasn't Clancy's fault.

Josh told me that after the paramedics pronounced Pat's death, they let Clancy have some time with him in the ambulance. After Clancy, Josh got a turn. He sat looking down at Pat's body and thought about how crazy this was. Lying before him was the strongest man he knew who could lift heavy building supplies and muscle massive equipment. And now he was gone. Josh told me that he and Pat had promised to take care of each other's families in case anything happened to them. He told me he intended to keep his promise.

Russ was there as well, talking to people when he could. Much of the time I saw him walking laps around the block.

More people arrived. My sister Barbara and her husband Doug flew in from Portland, Oregon. My sister Karla and her husband Andy arrived from Austin, Texas. Their kids flew in, as did an additional missionary from Loiyangalani named Tim Hines. I had no accurate sense of the passage of time. I felt that I couldn't take deep enough breaths. There just wasn't enough air. I also felt that I couldn't be alone and needed people around me. In a house filled with the people most important to me in the world—my kids, my parents, Pat's parents, all our brothers and sisters, nieces, nephews, friends and co-workers—I felt more alone than I've ever felt in my life. There was no amount of comfort or consoling that would make it better.

On Thursday afternoon, the day after the accident, we had an appointment at Olinger's Funeral Home to review plans for Pat's cremation and to review and sign papers. Russ had already discussed many of the details with the funeral director, but they needed me to come in person. I didn't want to be alone, so Russ, my dad, and my sisters agreed to come with me. It was getting close to the time of the appointment and my sister Barbara asked me when I wanted to leave for the funeral home.

All I could say was, "in about 45 years."

I didn't have that option. We left in about 20 minutes and soon found ourselves sitting around a shiny conference table in a quiet, carpeted room at the funeral home. It was excruciating going over detail after detail. We talked about planning for the memorial service, which would be that Saturday, October 9th at two o'clock. The funeral director was a woman who reminded me more of a caricature. She was tall and thin with medium length brown hair. Her name escapes me but it should have been Morticia. She threw her feet out in front of her body when she walked. She wore a plum polyester skirt suit and spoke with a slow monotone whine. This odd woman suggested that it might be a really good idea to get the person in charge of sound at our church record the service.

"My husband was the sound person," I yelled. There was no

one that I could think of who could jump in at the last minute and run the sound board. When we left the funeral home, I literally asked my family if that lady was for real. What a terrible time for a joke!

Somehow I made it through the appointment and back home to the house where people still gathered. Food piled up on a folding table someone had found and set up in the dining room. Lunch meats and bread, lasagna, pans of brownies, piles of cookies. Someone had set up coolers full of water bottles and soda. Soon, empty water bottles were scattered on every available surface of our house.

After it got dark, someone, maybe Clancy, decided they wanted to have one last Habana Night, which was a tradition Pat had started as part of the outreach of L2 Church. Although it was an activity Pat initiated and hosted, it was a form of outreach for both of us. We wanted people to understand that our faith was about our connection and service to others, whether or not they considered themselves Christians. Several years ago, Pat began hosting what he called Habana Nights. He invited groups of men over and they would sit on the patio in our backyard, smoking cigars and drinking beer. I helped him get the house ready and made the dinner.

Now, a number of these men—Clancy, Russ, Collin, and other friends Rich Wyatt, Seth Meisel, Ed Fuller, and others—pulled folding chairs out onto sparse grass on the side of the house and lit cigars and drank beer.

One by one, people drifted off and went home. I sat around a table in our dining room with my kids, my sisters, and their husbands and tried to figure out what to do next. We couldn't figure out where to go to sleep. Clancy's apartment felt cramped, but the Wolff house wouldn't hold all of us either. At 10:00 pm, my sisters booked a suite of rooms at the hotel where they were staying that would hold all of my kids and me. It helped knowing that my sisters and their families were nearby.

It felt good being in a small space with just my kids. That night, we all sat together on the hotel bed and talked. One by one, we all admitted that we didn't even feel like we wanted to keep living, that it felt like there was no good reason to go on. I read some scripture passages aloud, and we prayed and cried together. I knew that for all of them, I had to keep going.

There in that quiet hotel room, it felt like the first time since I had answered Josh's phone call that I could take a breath. One by one, my children all fell asleep. Finally, I did, too.

Chapter 6
Two Days Gone

Pat had been dead for two days. It still didn't seem real. Those first few moments when I woke in the morning and I hadn't yet remembered that Pat was gone were the best part of my day. Then it would hit me. Pat was dead. But was it a permanent situation? I would lie there in bed before I opened my eyes and think, with God ALL things are possible, right? I did believe that. Or at least I told everyone before this happened that I did. God could bring Pat back just as quickly as he took him. How would He do this? Simple. I'd just fall back asleep and when I woke up, it would all have been a dream.

Eventually, I would have to open my eyes. Where was God in all of this? How could this be God's plan? And, if we're supposed to be comforted and guided by God through grief, I certainly wasn't feeling it. All I felt was numb. This felt like more pain than I could handle, or wanted to handle. I think what was driving me to survive, even more than just survive, was that insanely protective mothering instinct. I had to make sure that my kids would get through this. It was my job. They shouldn't lose both of us.

By Friday, we all realized that there were details that needed attention, and which at least provided distraction for us. Pat and I had never talked about what we wanted if one of us should die suddenly. Honestly, I was certain that if that were to happen, it'd surely be me to go first and I really didn't care because I'd be dead. I knew that he would not want me to waste any money on a burial. I was prepared to ask my boys and Pat's brothers to throw together a plywood box. Russ took me outside and told me that in his opinion he thought that Pat would want me to do the least expensive thing. Cremation was what he suggested. Before, I had always been totally creeped out by the thought of my loved one melting in a furnace. Sort of a cross between Shadrach, Meshach, and Abednego in the fiery furnace and the Wicked Witch of the West in Wizard of Oz. Yet I had absolute faith in Russ to guide me so I agreed, but only if there could be a viewing first. I had yet to see him, and this was making me crazier by the minute. I needed to touch him and kiss him and tell him, at least his body, that I loved him. Russ communicated that to the right people and fought like mad to hurry the process along so that we could arrange the viewing and still have the service that same day while all the families were still in town. We could not push it off until the next week. I wouldn't survive that long waiting!

The Memorial Service had to be planned, including speakers and songs, a slide show and programs, and food for the hundreds of people we expected would show up. Someone took care of gathering photographs. Other people organized the potluck and the music. We knew that Russ, as the pastor of our church, would speak at the service, but talked about who else we could ask to say a few words. Someone had to write the obituary.

In addition, there were dismaying, practical details to handle. We had to figure out where Clancy's truck had been towed and what to do with it. Pat had a life insurance policy that we had to find and figure out how to process. Pat's business, so recently established, now had to be dismantled. Hundreds of tiny little decisions, any of which could have taken the better part of an afternoon to resolve, now piled up.

I felt powerless to address any of them. Many members of my family stepped in to help, to make phone calls, fill out reports, and track down details. I stood in the doorway of Pat's office, the one room we had made some effort to furnish, where Pat had carefully organized his files and his drawers. I still wanted to see my husband sitting at the desk in quiet concentration, working on our building plans, or entering billing statements on his computer. Instead, I saw several people scurrying around, scouring drawers looking for computer passwords, emptying files to find important documents. My two sisters seemed to be spurred into action. I think they needed to help as much as possible while they were both in Colorado. Their time with me would be short, so they buried their own sadness the best they could and quietly worked in Pat's office. That time spent in Pat's chair, and looking through his stuff, helped them know and understand him the way I did. I liked that. I wanted them to know more of what would now be missing for me: his meticulous bookkeeping, his saving and filing everything. It was an early sign to me of how part of the control over my life had been taken.

At some point, I felt I needed to get out of the house. I had a crazy thought: almost every woman that I loved surrounded me. I would not likely have that opportunity again any time soon. I was not working, so . . . . we should all go get pedicures. We should also have mimosas while having it done. I didn't realize how crazy that must have seemed at the time. Maybe this was denial. If I did something that I loved with the people I loved, maybe I'd be ok? Pat's sister Michele contacted a salon and arranged for all the girls to gather for pedicures. I decided to paint my nails an icy blue, the color of Pat's eyes.

I also realized that most of my dress clothes were in storage and I didn't have anything to wear to Pat's service. Tracy and Shell, Elizabeth, Sadie and a few others took me to a local mall to buy a black dress. I walked through Forever 21 thinking that everyone would be looking at me when I walked into the sanctuary. I'm fairly practical. I wanted a black dress that looked like me, but one I could wear again. I found a black knit dress I thought would work. As it turned out, I never did wear it again.

We were beginning to be asked how people could donate. Was there a memorial fund? It was all set up for me; all I needed to do was to go to the bank and sign the papers. I went to the bank where Pat had just recently set up his business accounts. It was a little office in the front of a grocery store. Just the week before, Pat had been dealing with one specific teller trying to order checks. He'd spent a long time with this teller. When I arrived at the bank that day to sign the papers, the same teller stood by his desk. He knew that I was Pat's wife and when he saw me walking toward him, he began to smile. I quickly told him that Pat had been killed in an accident. He immediately teared up. He apologized and excused himself. It was an early example to me of the great impact Pat had had on the people he interacted with in his everyday life.

When the banker returned he was very business-like and assisted us in getting everything arranged. We had to take Pat's name off of all our joint accounts. This was taking a while. While we were waiting, my phone rang. It was my sister, Karla. She had heard that the coroner's office in Lincoln County, where Pat's body was being held, wanted my permission to harvest Pat's corneas. I started sobbing in the middle of the bank. Of course, I said yes, but some crazy part in me balked. I still held out hope that God would undo Pat's death and bring him back to his body. I wondered, how would God work this miracle that I was not yet willing to rule out without Pat's corneas?

I let this thought go. Pat had absolutely amazing vision and I needed to share it with someone less fortunate, but it felt bitter, like fresh grief. I told the teller, one of Pat's newest friends, thank you and turned to leave. He stopped me and asked if it would be okay if he came to the memorial service. I gave the teller the information so that he could attend.

We got back to the house, now overflowing with flowers and piles of food. I hadn't had a haircut in months and my niece Elizabeth, a hair stylist, agreed to cut and color my hair in the kitchen of the Wolff house. I think we all just needed to be doing something, and this was something, all right—laughing and crying and choosing hair colors. If I remember correctly, I picked a nice shade of pink. Who was going to refuse me in that moment? It all seemed too strange. I remembered doing all of these things— nails, hair, new dress—when I married Pat. Now I was going through the same rituals as I prepared to say goodbye to him.

In the next room, my sisters Barbara and Karla were writing Pat's eulogy, which would also be published online as his obituary. A few years before, when my grandmother died, I'd mentioned how much I loved the fact that the pastor had drawn his remarks at her service almost entirely from the notes she had made in her bible, or verses she had underlined. So my sisters found Pat's Bible, which I had set on his desk, and started thumbing through it. They saw that he had highlighted one passage, thirteen verses from the book of Romans, and decided to structure Pat's eulogy around that.

Let love be genuine. Abhor what is evil; hold fast to what is good. Love one another with brotherly affection. Outdo one another in showing honor.

Do not be slothful in zeal, be fervent in spirit, serve the Lord. Rejoice in hope, be patient in tribulation, be constant in prayer.

Contribute to the needs of the saints and seek to show hospitality. Bless those who persecute you; bless and do not curse them. Rejoice with those who rejoice, weep with those who weep.

Live in harmony with one another. Do not be haughty, but associate with the lowly. Never be conceited. Repay no one evil for evil, but give thought to do what is honorable in the sight of all.

If possible, so far as it depends on you, live peaceably with all. . . . Do not be overcome by evil, but overcome evil with good.

Once they finished the main part of the eulogy, other people started contributing fun memories or funny stories that reminded them of Pat that they wanted included. Pat's parents and mine, our siblings, nieces and nephews, and children all had memories they wanted shared at the service or recorded in the online obituary.

And my memories? I was overwhelmed with memories of Pat, which stabbed at me. Everything my gaze took in led me to a memory. Everything that I heard or touched and every action carried my thoughts to a memory of him.

Once again, at the end of the day, people who had been keeping me and my kids company left for their own homes. We packed up for another night at the hotel. This would be the last day of the constant vigil at the Wolff house. There must be something built in us that seeks out the company of each other in the midst of tragedy, the longing for the physical presence of other people. I had needed the distraction, the reminder that there were people who were around me who loved me and still lived. I felt so empty and so very, very puzzled. What could God be accomplishing by all of this?

I still could not say that I felt the presence of God physically there with me in my grief. I received many cards telling me that God was with me always. They annoyed me. It seemed to me that others thought it was like driving alone in a car and I'd sense God buckled up in the passenger seat keeping me company. This didn't happen for me. When no one was with me, I felt so, so alone. But I began to recognize something that became even more apparent to me over time: God makes His presence known to us through the lives of other people. It was through all those people who walked single file through my tiny house, silently sat in chairs beside me, sorted through mail, brushed my hair or answered my phone calls that I was being shown the love and the care of God.

Chapter 7

Memorial

I woke up Saturday morning, impatient and nervous. It was going to be a big day. Pat's memorial service was scheduled for 2:00 p.m., which I knew would be emotional. In addition, we were scheduled to have Pat's viewing at the funeral home that morning before the service.

I couldn't wait to see him. Of course, I realized that it would only be Pat's body, not the actual man I knew and loved. Still, I was impatient to touch him, to be close to him, to see for myself that he was gone. It seemed wrong, unsettling, that he had been kept away from me. I wanted so badly to look at him, to see—however strange this seems—that he was okay. Part of me was nervous to see him that way, cold and unresponsive. Still, it was time for me to visit my husband.

We all drove over in several cars to the funeral home. Morticia, the funeral director, greeted us at the doors, but my sisters mercifully redirected her so I wouldn't have to talk with her. She had offered to let me have some time with Pat by myself before letting everyone else in the room, but at the time I thought that wouldn't be necessary. I don't remember how much time we had with him, but I knew it wasn't long. Looking back now, I wished I could have had unlimited time with him by myself. I still feel regret about this. At the time, however, I felt so fragile and uncomfortable being alone, especially in those first few days, that I wanted to have my kids and my family around me. I also wanted to be available for my kids when they visited. We were all unsure what to expect.

We walked through the door into the hushed silence of a large, dimly lit room. At the near end was a grouping of furniture, like a small sitting room with a red couch, coffee table and chairs. Vases filled with fake flowers sat on a side table. Framed prints of more flowers hung on the walls. A table at the far end of the room held snacks, coffee and water bottles. Against the long sidewall of the room was a fabric draped box. I walked up to it, my children and the rest of my family behind me.

There Pat lay, quiet and composed. He was wearing the clothes we'd picked out for him—jeans and his favorite pink paisley button-down shirt that he'd worn so many times. They'd tucked the shirt into his jeans, which seemed odd because he never wore it that way. I untucked the shirt, and he looked more normal. His head was shaved and bare, and other than a few scrape marks on his fingers from the accident, his body looked untouched. He had a small bruise on the bridge of his nose that I knew came from the Ambu bag used in the resuscitation attempt, along with a tiny scab on his lower lip that must have happened then also.

That was what, in fact, struck me the most: Pat looked just like Pat. He looked normal and handsome, like the man I had known every day for the past 28 years. The second I saw him, I exhaled deeply. Everyone and everything else fell away as I tried to soak up each inch of what he looked like. I held his face in my hands, trying to memorize every imperfection and the pores on his skin. I ran my fingers up and down his arms, held his hands, and took in the hair on the backs of his knuckles. I laid my head on his chest and felt the firmness of his muscles under my cheek. I looked and looked and looked. I even noticed the small skin tag on the end of his nose that he had asked me to pick on the day before the accident. It was so weird to see all the evidences of our shared life together, still evident, still visible. How can it be over? I wish now that I had taken even more time just to be with Pat and stare at his face, but I felt that the time was short and I knew that everyone else would want to have time with him as well. I stepped away, and invited our children to come closer.

The kids all stepped up to see him, and my focus shifted to helping them get through this moment with some sort of peace. I knew it was my job to get them through it. Sadie had said she wasn't sure she would be able to do it, but she stood next to her father, crying. Jesse and Clancy stood nearby, their hands in their pockets. James, who had decided to come to the viewing in his pajama pants, with no objection from me, stood right by my side.

"It's okay," I said. "It's just Dad. See?"

I think we all expected him to be blue, or not look like himself. I ran my fingers over the cool skin of his hands.

"It's just like he's been out shoveling snow in the cold," I said. "It's okay. It's still Dad. He still feels like Dad."

I stepped back and let other people have time with him. I even had to laugh when one of our nieces, Molly, said "Leave it to Uncle Pat to look this good." Relieved that I felt okay seeing Pat's body, I was able to mingle and talk with everyone who had come. I completely understood that some people didn't feel up to the viewing, but I was surprised that it provided a sort of peace and calm that I'd been missing. I was glad I had come. I suddenly understood the thinking behind holding a wake, people talking and eating and spending one last hour with the person who had died.

Eventually, our time was up. We had requested that my kids and I have the last fifteen or twenty minutes with Pat by ourselves. The five of us stood next to Pat, staring at his face for the final time. I wasn't sure how we would ever be able to walk away from him. It seemed wrenching to tear my eyes away. I needed to be strong for myself and my children. Eventually, we huddled together, and I prayed aloud:

"Dear God, please give us the courage to walk away from Pat's body and to be faithful. In Jesus name we pray, Amen."

And then I told the kids that I would count to three and we would all turn around and walk away. Sort of like pushing each other out of the airplane. We linked arms.

One, two, three.

Arm in arm we all marched out of the door, out of the funeral home, and to the car. The moment I uttered "Amen," I felt like the role of being head of the house, provider and protector, transferred from Pat to me.

When we got home, we changed for the memorial service. I had my new black dress to wear and hung the chain with Pat's wedding ring around my neck. I carried Pat's Bible. Each of the kids wore one of Pat's shirts. Even Seth, a young man who was an honorary member of our family, had one of Pat's shirts. The boys wore theirs untucked, just as Pat did, and Sadie wore hers belted over a skirt. Jesse wore Pat's boots, the ones I had stumbled over in our bedroom. (He has continued to wear Pat's boots, his jeans, and his shirts. He even just recently had one pair of boots resoled.)

We drove to L2 Church where the service was held. Jesse drove by himself because he wanted to drive Pat's truck and park it in its usual spot. We all gathered in a lower room with the rest of the family waiting to be led into the auditorium at the start of the service. There must have been forty people, all immediate relatives of mine or Pat's, waiting together. I sat in a chair, feeling nervous for those who were going to speak.

We climbed a short flight of stairs and entered the sanctuary, a large sloping room that in its previous life had served as a Christian Science building. It had seats for just under 500 people. I looked up into the rows of people and saw that every single seat was taken. Extra chairs had been set up in the lobby behind the sanctuary. People crowded in the aisles, sitting or standing on the stairs. The number of people who showed up on two days' notice overwhelmed me. Who were all of these people? It was easily the largest gathering of people the church had ever seen.

We all went to sit in the rows of seats that had been left open for our family. My kids and I sat in the front row, my kids to the left of me, my mother on my right. I settled in, clutching Pat's Bible to my chest, intending to take in and remember as much of this service as I could, just as I had, hours before, tried to take in every inch of my husband's face.

I was successful. Years later, I still have very clear memories of that service, an unusual island of clarity standing out against the fog and disconnected feeling of those first months. I wanted this service to be a break from the sadness and mourning that had overwhelmed our lives in recent days, and more of a celebration of Pat's life.

We had three speakers. Russ gave a short message. He was strong and steady. He spoke to each of my four children one at a time as if the 750 other people were not in the room. He challenged them to not let this event define them.

Josh Bard talked about the sovereignty of God. He spoke of how unbelievably strong Pat was. He shared how he, being a pro baseball player, had witnessed many strong athletic men, yet Pat was the strongest man of his age that he'd ever known. Still his life was so fragile. This was evidence to him of God's perfect timing.

Finally, Jim Teasdale, the missionary from Africa, shared stories about the time Pat and I had spent the month with them in Kenya and the work Pat had contributed there. He spoke of our fishing expeditions on Lake Turkana and how, in spite of Pat's best efforts, everyone else caught fish except Pat.

After the speakers, Pat's brothers Steve and Dave read the prepared eulogy and shared favorite memories of their brother. And then there was the slideshow that a friend had put together. I sat beside my children and watched as picture after picture of Pat's heart-stopping blue eyes, smiling face—dimples showing, teeth gleaming—filled the huge screen at the front of the sanctuary.

And we sang. Although I was unable to sing again for many, many months, I completely gave myself up to the music of those songs. We sang "I'll Fly Away" . . .

One bright morning when this life over, I'll fly away.
To a place on God's celestial shore, I'll fly away.
When I die, hallelujah, by and by,
I'll fly away.

I imagined Pat flying to heaven, seeing Jesus face to face. This was not singing about a notion of times to come. This was the reality of what had happened to the person who was flesh of my flesh.

At the end of the service, Russ shared that he and Pat had often talked about how the most important part of their ministries was to have made a difference in people's lives. They had often thought it would be interesting to know, at the end of their lives, what kind of impact they had made. They thought it would be intriguing if, at either of their funerals, people whose lives they had impacted would be asked to stand. Russ said he always assumed that he would die first, and so this experiment would start with him. Never had he thought he would have the opportunity to ask people whether or not Pat had ministered to them.

This was his chance. Standing before an overflowing sanctuary, he asked that anyone who had felt that their lives had been affected by Patrick McKendry would simply stand. I stood, along with my children, and we turned and looked up at the packed room. Hundreds of people were standing. There was the person at the 7-11 store Pat saw everyday when he bought his coffee before work. There was the bank teller. There were people that he played softball with. It was overwhelming and humbling. Pat was a quiet man who mostly worked behind the scenes. Still, it was powerful evidence of the impact one person can have by simply paying attention to the people you come across every day. It was one of the most moving moments of my life, and I was grateful.

After the service, we all went out to the steps in front of the church and released balloons. I watched them fly away, getting caught by the wind. They got smaller and smaller, until they were tiny dots against the clear, blue sky.

There was a huge reception in the basement of the church afterward, put together mostly by my friend Corrie Casey and a group of hardworking people who somehow in a few days organized the effort to feed hundreds of people. There were so many people to see, and so many people who wanted to see me. I appreciated everyone who came and made an effort to reach out to my family and me.

That said, I also appreciated the fact the Corrie also acted as my protector. She made sure I had food and something to drink. She also made sure I had an opportunity to take a break from meeting people occasionally, helping me find a side room where I could sit quietly and gather my strength.

After a while, people said goodbye, got in their cars and went home. We had mourned Pat's death, and remembered and cele-brated his life. I was still so far away from knowing how to go forward without him, but it was time to move on. We gathered up all the bouquets of flowers people had sent and the portraits of Pat that we'd displayed in the lobby and went back to the Wolff house.

My sisters and their families were scheduled to fly home the next day, and this would be the last night we would all have together. We started cleaning up the house, throwing away empty water bottles and food containers, stacking up the folding chairs and tables, and putting the house back to something like normal. It hit me again just how derelict and unfinished the house was.

I stood at the kitchen sink, my hands in dirty dishwater scrubbing a pot, wondering what we would do with the house. I had never minded living through construction before. I could always live with the bare stud walls and stripped flooring and questionable plumbing because I knew Pat could make it beautiful. I would have been able to put up with washing dishes in a chipped sink with bad water pressure, or putting them away in crooked cabinets that smelled like mildew because I knew they were only temporary until Pat replaced them.

I also knew that the boys wanted to finish the house themselves, perhaps as a way to carry on their father's work. They were becoming accomplished builders and had many of the skills necessary, but I knew they had their own lives to figure out, and other work to do. Even more, standing in that kitchen, I knew I couldn't do it. I couldn't make it through the winter in that house. Not for the first time, I thought it would have been so much easier if God had taken me instead of Pat.

I started crying. My sister Barbara saw me and put her arm around my shoulders.

"What's wrong?" she asked.

"I can't do it," I said. "I can't live here. I can't finish this house."

"Then don't," she said. "You have options. You can find an apartment until you figure things out."

Within an hour, I had talked it over with my sisters, my parents, and my kids. As hard as it was to let go of the Wolff house and the dream it represented, we all agreed that we had to move on to a different future. We had to figure out a "new normal" for ourselves.

CHAPTER 8
A NEW NORMAL

In those first few days, weeks and months, I talked often with my kids about the fact that what had seemed like normal life to us was gone forever. We knew that nothing would ever be the same again. We had so loved this man who had been central to our lives, and now he was gone. There was no way to fill this hole in our lives. And to be honest, none of us would want to. We didn't want *not* to miss him; we wanted him back. I believe this is part of the healing power of grief. Having the pain of his loss was one way to continue to feel our connection to him, no matter how hard.

And it was hard. Outwardly, I took all the steps to keep our family moving in the right direction. We had decided to enlist the help of our families and community to get the Wolff house cleaned up enough that we could sell it. My kids and I would move somewhere else while the work was being done. Once the decision was made to move out of the Wolff house, I then had to decide where we would move. We had several options. Josh and Lindsey offered to let us live with them in Castle Rock, about 30-40 minutes from where we were. My sister Barbara and her husband Doug offered to help us relocate near where they lived in Oregon, which was the only other place Pat and I ever thought about moving. But moving away from the area didn't feel right. Denver was where my kids had their lives and schools. Denver was where I had my job and my community. I knew I would stay. But where?

Clancy already had his apartment in Arvada near where we had lived before moving to the Wolff house. We considered renting a larger, or even a second apartment in his complex. I drove with my parents to check out the apartment on Monday, but learned that there were no apartments available in that complex.

Another option that appealed to me was to be somewhere near Russ and Tracy. When they sold the house that had been down the street from us in Arvada, they moved to a condo in East Denver, just blocks away from L2 Church. Their children were grown and they wanted to downsize. They sold a car and Russ walked to his office at the church. There was an apartment complex next door to their condo building. It was small, but clean, and would allow our two dogs. I also wouldn't have to worry about shoveling snow, mowing lawns, or maintaining a house. I decided that this was where we needed to be. It had just two bedrooms, so Jesse and James would share a room and Sadie would sleep with me. This worked out anyway. I found that I slept badly, if at all, in an empty bed. Jesse and James were a 20-minute drive from their schools, and Sadie would be much closer to her college from this new location. Tracy worked at my office and we could carpool most days. Apartment living was a far cry from where I expected to find myself living at this point in my life, but I needed to go back to something that felt familiar. Having Russ and Tracy nearby so I could join them for morning coffee or an evening glass of wine felt good to me.

Some of the dentists from my office wrote checks to cover six months' rent on the apartment as a way to give me some breathing room while we figured out our lives. I signed the lease and we arranged to move into the apartment the following weekend.

I stayed home from work that first week. There were still so many details that I needed to sort out, from getting the death certificate to closing accounts, meetings with estate attorneys and the Department of Social Services. I pushed myself to get tasks checked off my list and, at the end of the day collapsed in tears and exhaustion.

One morning that week, Jesse and James had gone to school and Sadie was not yet home from her labs. I was alone in the house. Suddenly, a wave of grief came over me, and I just felt that I couldn't be in my skin. I felt achy and uncomfortable, and decided that I might feel better if I took a bath. I filled the tub and sank into the water. It didn't help. I felt panicky and claustrophobic. I couldn't breathe. I crawled out of the tub and wrapped myself in a towel, feeling helpless. I laid on the cold floor, spent. I reached for my phone and texted Lindsey Bard, a person with whom I would continue to have a close emotional connection during that time and beyond.

"I can't breathe," I typed onto my phone. "I don't think I have the courage to get up off the floor of the bathroom." I don't remember exactly what she texted back, but I do remember that a response was immediate, and I recall that she began praying at that moment. I didn't feel less pain. I wasn't any more sure of the future, but I did get up off the floor. Was this the attendance of God? Was it normal? Was I crazy? Was I always going to feel this way? I almost didn't recognize myself.

But, as I learned over those first few weeks, the pain couldn't actually kill me. I got through the days, through the tasks, through the grief. What was the alternative to getting through?

Through all of this, running in the background, was the support of my parents. Each day they got in their car and took the hour-long drive to Denver to do whatever they needed to do. And I needed them. Everyone else went back to their daily lives, or tried to. Not my parents. They had been a principal support to Pat and me for years, providing childcare and after school support for our kids, helping with the housework while both Pat and I worked full time. For the past several years they had driven to Denver twice a week to help keep our lives running smoothly. We were more grateful for them than they could ever know, and they were central figures in our lives. Just that year, with Jesse driving, our moving further away to the Wolff house, and our kids getting older, they were planning to slow down some, limiting their trips to Denver to once each week.

And then Pat died.

Everything they had planned was put on hold to help my children and me. They had booked and paid for an 11-day trip to the Holy Land for later in October, a dream trip my father especially had looked forward to for years. My mother initially decided that they just would not go. They offered to have us move in with them in Berthoud. When I decided I wanted to stay in Denver, they offered to get an apartment in Denver to be closer to us. They were so sad that Pat, their son-in-law, whom they had known since we were teenagers, was gone. They were even more grief-stricken that this tragedy had befallen their youngest child.

As a parent myself, I understand something of this feeling. When your kids are hurting, there is nothing you won't do to help. In the coming months, I would be given an opportunity to see my own protective instincts rise up in defense of my own child. My parents, especially my mother, were no different. This was the same woman who had gone toe-to-toe with administrators in my elementary school when they weren't acting quickly enough to provide support for my learning disabilities. My mother, a fairly quiet woman who prefers small groups to crowds, would become a warrior when it came to protecting or assisting her children.

In addition, she was already too well acquainted with grief over the past many years, She had nursed her mother-in-law, my paternal grandmother, through Alzheimer's disease until her death in 2002. Then she had nursed her own mother through surgeries and illnesses until she died in 2006. She was close to both of her brothers, Bill and Earl, and was heartbroken when she learned that Bill had lung cancer. She visited him frequently until his death in 2007, which was followed shortly after by the death from cancer of her remaining brother Earl only nine months later, in 2008. She had waded through grief and known it all too well. After Pat's accident, it seemed that she felt she needed to take some sort of action against the powerlessness of death.

My parents rushed in, trying to fill in the gaps of what was missing in my life. They ferried James back and forth from school, helping him with his homework. My mother did laundry and housework and grocery shopping. My father began to schedule and meet with all the volunteers for the Wolff house remodel. He bought the necessary supplies and was the extra hand everyone needed. They helped me pack boxes—again—and get ready for the move to the new apartment. They were tireless and dedicated, and I'm sure that my kids and I, in our exhausted, shocked states, were not able to show them the kind of appreciation they deserved. But even more than that, I think they were trying to find a way to help us be okay, something that wouldn't happen for any of us for a long time. It was, in part, their task to just be with us in our sadness without being able to fix it, as much as they wanted to. They saw close up how hard it was for all of us to move on. It must have been heartbreaking for them.

One week after Pat's memorial service, we moved to the new apartment. In addition to my parents and Russ and Tracy, we had a crew of probably 20 people, all friends and family, who helped us move. My good friend Kelly and my sisters-in-law helped me pack up our closet. They brought over wardrobe boxes for Pat's clothes so they could be stored nicely until I could decide what to do with them (and where they have remained ever since). As I lifted his shirts and pants off the closet rod, I imagined seeing him in each of them. The grief was so overwhelming that I crumpled to the floor a few times. These courageous women just stayed glued to me on all sides. If I went down, they went down, too. I think this task took the longest of all. When we were done, the house was empty. We had not moved all that much in as we prepared for an extensive remodel, but this amazing crew moved me out of the Wolff house and into the apartment by noon that same day. Everything was packed and transported, unpacked and set up in about four hours.

By Saturday evening, my newly diminished family was relocated into the apartment. Beds were made, groceries filled the refrigerator, and pictures hung on the wall. This would be home, at least for a while. I was relieved to be in a place that was clean and with the constant protection of Russ and Tracy next door. We had space to ourselves when we needed to be alone, but could run next door at any moment if we suddenly felt panicked. I knew that Russ would protect me but also encourage me to live responsibly in light of my faith.

There was a year-round outdoor saltwater swimming pool and hot tub as part of the apartment complex, unusual in Colorado. In the days to come, the pool would provide us with something to do after school and work. None of us really enjoyed watching television, and listening to music stirred up too much emotion. In the evening, I would sink into the warm, salty water of the hot tub and watch James swim and play in the pool. It was good for both of us.

Sometime during the move someone asked me, almost in passing, if I'd thought about getting an attorney for Clancy. A close friend told me, just hours after the accident, that I should consider it, but I'd dismissed the question. An attorney? For what? Clancy had done nothing wrong. He hadn't even been given a ticket at the scene of the accident, even though the deputy had questioned

Clancy at length. Besides, hadn't he suffered enough loss? Wasn't losing his father a significant enough consequence for Clancy to face?

I pushed the thought from my mind. It seemed crazy. In just ten days, our family had faced the most terrible situation possible. Surely the worst was behind us. Reasonable people in positions of authority would surely recognize how dangerous this stretch of road was, wouldn't they? Certainly, they would want to change the road to make it safer. Why would anyone want to pin Pat's death on his innocent son?

CHAPTER 9
MOVING ON

It was the first dream about Pat I'd had since he'd died. I was in a huge field that felt in some way like an epic battlefield, something I might have seen in the movie *Gladiator*. Everything was sepia colored, with dry grass underfoot and buildings that looked like Roman ruins. The field was filled with people and I was looking for Pat. There was something wrong between us and I knew that if I could just get close to him, if I could just talk to him, we could find a way to fix this horrible situation. I ran through the crowds searching for him. I would just catch a glimpse of him in the distance and scramble to reach him, frantically pushing people out of my way. Yet, just as I drew close to him, he would move away from me. "Pat," I would yell, "I just have to talk to you," but he wouldn't stop. He just kept walking away.

I woke up feeling frustrated and panicky. In those early days, especially in quiet, unguarded moments, I was often overcome with the feeling that there just had to be a way to change the outcome of the accident. Waking up from this dream, I felt that Pat was slowly slipping away from me, from our marriage, and I struggled, even against all the available information, to get him back.

Of course, I wasn't successful. I'd get out of bed, dress for work, and get myself and the kids out of the door. I tried to figure out on a daily basis how I was going to reconfigure a life without Pat that made sense.

The fact that we were living in a completely new environment, one in which Pat had never been a part, made the transition both easier and harder. I quickly realized that every one of Pat's possessions, every piece of his clothing, every scrap of paper with his handwriting on it, carried a memory of him. I imagined that had we still been living in the house in Arvada where we'd lived for fifteen years, Pat's memories would have inhabited every square foot of the place. I wouldn't have been able to drive into the garage, dust the furniture or open a closet without being reminded of Pat's presence. The kids and I were still flooded with memories and longings for him, but we were less likely to stumble across an object that might catch us unprepared.

Instead, we intentionally carried reminders of Pat into the new apartment with us. We'd had family portraits done a few years earlier and the photographer graciously allowed us to reprint several of them in larger sizes to display at Pat's memorial service. Now these photos were hung on the walls of the apartment, including one of Pat and me I had hung over my bed. One evening, Sadie and I laid on the bed, our heads at the foot and our stockinged feet resting on the pillows, and just stared at the photograph, remembering Pat's skin and how he'd get ingrown hairs on his head from shaving his scalp bald. We reexamined his dimples and the little smile lines around his eyes.

Jesse now drove Pat's truck. The boys had also brought over a few of his shirts and his boots, which they all took turns wearing, and which helped them feel connected to him. I still wore Pat's wedding ring on a chain around my neck and had his camo beanie that he'd taken with him the day of the accident. And, of course, I had Pat's Bible. Other than that, I had few tangible belongs that would remind me of my absent husband on a daily basis.

Which is of course what also made it hard. I found myself yearning for any physical connection I could find. I wanted to inhale his scent on some of his clothing, but most of his clothes had been stored in the smelly closets of the Wolff house, so my mom had washed most of the clothes and there wasn't anything that still smelled like him. I had heard from other widows that they had found comfort in favorite objects, special pieces of clothing, but because of the timing of our moves—three times in six months—I was without many of Pat's possessions. I didn't feel like I could to sink into my grief, or wallow in it. I sometimes wondered why. Maybe God was saying, "You have to trust me. You have to continue on."

I woke up every morning, listening for the sound of Pat movements in the bathroom, the music that had accompanied my mornings for years. Pat was meticulous and detailed in all of his activities. He established systems and routines that worked for him and never varied from them. He got up the same time every day and got ready for work in a particular order. Over the years, I had memorized the precise way he shaved his head or washed his face. I knew exactly the sound of his morning routine and used it as my alarm.

Of course, these new mornings in the apartment had a different rhythm, one without Pat's routine. I soon realized that part of my job in moving on without Pat was learning to come to terms with a life of compromise. For example, the last step of Pat's morning routine was to take his towel, damp from the bath, and wipe down the countertops, the sinks and the mirrors. After even a week in the new apartment, I noticed that the sinks and the countertops were dirtier, and the mirrors stayed splattered.

The sense of compromise expanded to other parts of the house. No matter what condition any of our homes were ever in, I knew Pat could always make it better. If I was drawn to a new style of decorating, he could build anything to make it look like a picture I had seen. When we were looking for the house in Arvada, we learned that the real estate flyer had a misprint, indicating that there was a basement when there was not. Pat asked me, "Is this the place you want to live? If so, I can do an addition with a basement. I'll match the brick so it doesn't look like an add on." And that's exactly what he did.

After we finished remodeling that house, I searched for nearly six months for an entertainment center that would hold our large, freestanding television. I finally found a picture in a magazine of what I wanted. We learned it was a high-end piece of furniture that cost $45,000 - $50,000 to buy. Pat looked at the picture and then custom-built one that looked even better than the one in the picture for a few hundred dollars. It was so lovely that when we finally went to sell, the realtor said that the cabinet would be the biggest selling point and suggested we leave it. It was my favorite of all the things Pat had ever built for me, but I left it with the house, thinking that he could always build me another one.

Now, I was excruciatingly aware of how much more limited my options were. I couldn't expect to build the house I wanted. Even more, I would have to lower my standards for even maintaining the house I was in. Before, if the sink leaked, Pat could repair it. Now, when something broke in the apartment, which happened with a frequency that was alarming for a new apartment building, I had to wait for the maintenance person to come and make the repair. Often, it wouldn't be fixed to the standards Pat would have demanded. Many times, Jesse—trained by Pat—would come along behind the maintenance crew and fix it himself.

In addition, I noticed my inclination to watch out for the "worst-case scenario." When the worst possible thing has happened, you begin to assume that if anything else bad can happen, it will happen to you. One night while walking back from Russ and Tracy's building to our apartment on a path that took us through the parking garage of our apartment building, we noticed that water was leaking from an apartment on the floor above us.

"That has to be our apartment that's flooded," said Sadie, watching the water drip from the concrete overhead.

In fact, it wasn't our apartment that was flooded. The bad thing hadn't happened to us this time. Still, it was interesting to notice my automatic assumption that all bad things happened to me. I was constantly bracing myself for more bad news.

By the beginning of November, I had made strides in recognizing the big ways my life had changed—my husband, co-parent, lover, and financial partner was gone—but I began to appreciate the little ways in which things would be different going forward. I actively looked for ways to cope and to find some sense of comfort and control.

So what helped?

Strangely, for me, books. Given a lifetime of struggling with learning disabilities, reading had never been a favorite pastime. But this was a new world. When I got home from work, after making and eating dinner, I found I wasn't comfortable watching television. Every single show seemed to be about a great love story, which was hard to watch, or about the loss of a great love—equally hard. The same was true of movies. Music, which Pat and I had always enjoyed, was a minefield for memories. A song could come on and sucker punch me into grief. To fill the empty time between dinner and actual sleep, I turned to books, specifically books by people dealing with grief. I read the stories of women who had lost their husbands, husbands who had lost their wives, parents who had lost their children. It was helpful in two ways. First, I found words that expressed the very things I was feeling. I wasn't crazy! Other people had had the same irrational, depressed thoughts and had lived to write about it. I found a companionship with people I had never met, and felt a closeness to them I wouldn't have thought possible.

Secondly, these words gave me a way to share with other people what I was experiencing. I would be reading a book in the lunchroom at my office and come across a particular passage that rang true for me. I'd read it out loud to my co-workers around me and it felt good to be able to share how I was feeling in a way that other people could understand. It gave me my first inkling of how powerful a book could be, and the first idea that I might someday want to share my own experiences in writing.

The next thing I learned was an idea I got from one of the books I read. In it, there was a story about a woman with nine children. She worked on an assembly line bagging rice to make ends meet. When someone asked her how she did it all, her answer was, "I do the next thing that needs to be done."

Do the next thing that needs to be done. This was a shattering, welcome realization to me. Going through such an emotional upheaval, there is a panic to get the future figured out, planned out, all right now. But in my clearer moments, I realized that I didn't have to figure it all out. I just had to figure out the next five minutes. This was my daily plan. Just break it down. Only focus on the decisions I have to make today. I really wish I had remembered this more, because it helped. When I found myself feeling overwhelmed, I would try to allow myself just to make the decisions necessary for that day. That decision may be as simple as what to have for dinner. It could be as big as the decision to move to the apartment near Russ and Tracy. I didn't know what my life would look like in five years, ten years, or twenty years. I just had to figure out what worked for me that day.

Another thing that felt good to me, strangely, was working. I had gone back to work at the dentist office within ten days of the accident, in part because I needed the income, but just as importantly, I needed the structure of work and the support of the people I worked with. As I've said, Tracy worked at the same office with me several days a week, and it was good to be able to drive in with her. In addition, my co-workers were friends, people I had known for years. Collectively we had been through several divorces, the death of a grandchild, and sudden illnesses. We experienced unexpected children from multiple births to adoptions to teen pregnancy. Every day, our lunch hours were spent solving the most pressing conflict or, at the very least, relating to each other and sharing ideas.

In many small ways, by November our lives were settling in and the kids and I got back into the requirements of work and school. My parents came up frequently, with my mom helping with laundry, errands, and monitoring James' schoolwork. The work had started in earnest on the Wolff house. We got bark collars for the dogs, who were unused to the noise and commotion of an apartment, but eventually they, too, calmed down. This was about as close to settled as things were likely to be for a while.

Which gave me more time to think. I realized early on that I needed to pay attention to what was going on inside my own head. I had learned that the way I felt had a lot to do with what I was thinking. It would be easy to get lost in the sad, sad story that was never too far from my present mind: *My life won't ever be good again. I won't be able to cope. The kids would be better off if I had died instead of Pat.* It felt like I was running on a slippery floor, and it was all too easy to fall into grief. I knew these thoughts were not true, but they had the power to make me feel desperate and scared. I needed better thoughts—words I knew were true and which gave me comfort and courage.

As a Christian, the obvious choice was to fill my mind with scripture. There was a verse I saw that Pat had starred in his Bible, which addressed this very idea:

> *I appeal to you therefore brothers by the mercies of God to present your bodies as a living sacrifice holy and acceptable to God which is your spiritual worship. Do not be conformed to this world, but be transformed by the renewal of your mind that by testing you may discern what is the will of God, what is good and acceptable and perfect.*

This passage wasn't new to me. I had memorized it many years before, thinking it would be relevant in child rearing and counseling others through their struggles. Now it was requiring much from me in my darkest hours, telling me how I needed to approach my grief. I would have to be responsible for my thoughts and to transform them with scripture. I also felt that having invested so many years in studying the Bible and learning from it, it was now available to me as a resource from which I could draw, like drinking water from a well I had filled over decades.

One of the benefits of living near Russ and Tracy, and one of the factors in my choice to move near them, was that I wanted and needed Russ's spiritual support. Russ could remind me on a regular basis of the truths I was determined to live by. I already knew the scripture. I already believed it to be true, but I knew I was required to affirm it. I just felt it was helpful to have other people quoting it to me. Josh Bard performed this service for me and would quote scripture to me for fifteen minutes at a time. More often, however, it was Russ and Tracy who helped me shout down the despair and anger that raged in my mind. I would go over to their house in the mornings before work, still wearing my pajamas. Many, many evenings, we would go over after dinner (or quite often, join them for dinner), and Russ and I would sit on their balcony despite the cold, and just talk. It didn't instantly make me feel happy, or that my situation was resolved or even fine, but it did feel like I was taking a positive step to take care of my kids and myself.

In the midst of all of this, I started to wonder what my new ministry should or could be. My sense of service had always been so intertwined with Pat's service. Together we felt we had a ministry to the world through our marriage, through our family, through our work, and through our church. But with Pat gone, what was I supposed to do going forward? Not only had I lost my partner and my familiar life, I lost a sense of my own identity as well.

I stood on the balcony with Russ and Tracy, slowly sipping a glass of wine, looking out at the silhouette of the Rocky Mountains in the distance. I listened as Russ encouraged me to actively apply verse after verse to my situation, including these from Isaiah 65:

See, I will create new heavens and a new earth.

The former things will not be remembered, nor will they come to mind.

But be glad and rejoice forever in what I will create, for I will create Jerusalem to be a delight and its people a joy.

I will rejoice over Jerusalem and take delight in my people; the sound of weeping and of crying will be heard in it no more.

Never again will there be an infant who lives but a few days, or an old man who does not live out his years; the one who dies at a hundred will be thought a mere child; the one who fails to reach a hundred will be considered accursed.

They will build houses and dwell in them; they will plant vineyards and eat their fruit.

No longer will they build houses and others live in them, or plant and others eat.

For as the days of a tree, so will be the days of my people; my chosen ones will long enjoy the work of their hands.

They will not labor in vain, nor will they bear children doomed to misfortune; for they will be a people blessed by the Lord, they and their descendants with them.

Before they call I will answer; while they are still speaking I will hear.

Russ had once done a sermon on heaven that stayed with me. He said that the work we are doing here on earth is preparing us for what we'll do in heaven. I could see Pat's life crescendoing to this heavenly career. Maybe Pat, after his lifetime of work as a master builder and craftsman, had been called to heaven to build beautiful houses there. I found comfort in the thought, knowing the types of havens he was able to create.

I also knew that I, left behind, did not want to labor in vain. I was pretty sure there wouldn't be dental decay in heaven where my services would be needed. But what, I wondered, would I be called to do?

CHAPTER 10

THANKSGIVING

This was the first major holiday for our family without Pat. For simplicity and continuity, we decided to have Thanksgiving dinner with the large McKendry clan. Pat's sister Michelle and her husband were hosting the meal at their house, but everyone brought food. We had traditionally had a deep-fried turkey, and, of course, Pat was the person who usually undertook this important task. This year, our nephew Jon was designated as the turkey fryer. He did a good job and the turkey tasted great, but I found it hard to accept that the baton had been passed. It was one more reminder that our future would look so different from what I had known.

I'm not sure what I expected the holiday to feel like, but it was no surprise to me that it was hard. I sat at the table after dinner, eating pie and feeling more and more discontent. It felt less like grief and more like I just couldn't find a way to be comfortable.

I watched my children interact with all the aunts and uncles and cousins. On the surface, everything was fine, but my sense was that underneath the surface, there was tension and turmoil.

I overheard some of the kids talking about a goose-hunting trip that the boys were taking the next day. These hunting trips were always an adventure for Pat and the boys and he had always made sure that everyone had everything they'd need for the trip. But this time it became apparent—at 9:00 on Thanksgiving night—that without Pat's guidance, James didn't have the gear he needed. He was a growing 14-year-old boy and had outgrown all the gear he'd used the year before.

Of all my sons, James is the least enthusiastic about hunting. He was much more motivated by baseball and usually went along on the hunting trips to spend time with his brothers, cousins, and his dad. I halfway expected him to just say that he wouldn't go on the trip, but for some reason he seemed more determined than ever to be included.

That's when everything fell apart. I felt guilty that I hadn't thought ahead about the hunting trip, anticipating that James might have outgrown his gear. This had been a duty I'd always handed off to Pat, so the thought never crossed my mind. I felt completely inadequate and overwhelmed nonetheless.

At the same time, everyone came down pretty hard on James, lecturing him that he should have taken more responsibility and taken care of this on his own. I knew that James would have to learn to handle future situations like this, but I felt it was unfair to expect him to come up to speed so quickly. I just wanted everyone, anyone, to cut us some slack. I started crying. I gathered my kids and our coats and empty dishes and left. Somehow, we survived the day. Somehow, people helped James pull together a set of hunting gear for the next day. I'm sure it wasn't pretty, and probably didn't fit particularly well, but it was enough. I decided that "enough" was the standard I would live with for a while.

I think that part of the underlying tension on that Thanksgiving Day was that I had started to worry again about Clancy and the possibility that the district attorney could still charge him for the accident. None of it made any sense to me or to Clancy, but I had heard murmurings that they hadn't closed the file. I couldn't dismiss the worry so I had called the clerk at Lincoln county a few times to check the status in hopes to get some information that would ease my mind. The lack of answers made me fear that the worst wasn't, in fact, over. Was there more to come? It was hard to move forward when I weren't sure about what my future would require of me.

Clancy, for the most part, worked to find his footing again. He had taken a break from school and, without his dad's business, was without a job. He was also living in an apartment by himself, so he did not have the built-in support of his family to help him get through the day. In the back of his mind, he also was worried about being charged. In addition to the unfairness of being accused of something for which he did not believe he was guilty, being charged would carry additional career consequences for him. Although he had started college intending to major in music, he was quickly drawn to the field of criminal justice. He liked the idea of working for justice for people, and being one of the "good guys." He had worked in security for our church and for the many other events that took place in the church building. He also had extensive firearms training, in addition to all his years of hunting with his dad. The active lifestyle of a police officer appealed to him, as did the idea of being in public service. His plan, after taking a break in the fall to work with Pat on our house, was to enroll in a Police Officer Standards and Training (POST) program in the winter. Ironically, even the experience of the accident itself had confirmed his belief that he was on the right track. Many people thought that after being at the scene of an accident where his father died he would never be able to work in such a stressful situation again. Instead, he learned that he did have the resources and the emotional ability to handle emergencies. More than ever, this was what he wanted to do.

Unfortunately, with either a misdemeanor or felony conviction on his record, he would not be able to drive any sort of emergency vehicle. His career aspirations as a police officer would end with any conviction. Knowing this, Clancy had for years made the tough choices to keep away from situations that could get him into trouble. He would not attend parties where there was underaged drinking. He avoided contact with people who might be using drugs. He made an effort to have a good relationship with his teachers in high school and college. I'm sure he wondered if all of that effort and attention would now be for nothing. His future dangled from a string held in someone else's hands.

Everything was in limbo. With no job and months to go before he could even think about the POST training, he had no obvious structure to fill his time. Fortunately, a young man named David Fox lived a couple of blocks away from his apartment.

David and Clancy didn't know each other well, and had only hung out together a couple of times before that fall, but they had talked about hunting together sometime. Ironically, the first time David called to invite Clancy hunting was the night before Pat's memorial service. David ran in different circles and had not heard about the accident. He felt terrible calling, and felt bad for Clancy. He promised he would get back in touch in a week or so.

David followed through. About ten days later, he called and invited Clancy to go duck hunting. Clancy agreed. What David didn't know was how nervous Clancy was about hunting again. Clancy had rarely gone hunting without Pat. In addition, it was their favorite thing they did together. Even though they'd spent lots of time building together, or playing softball, being out hunting gave Clancy his favorite memories of his dad. Going out with David would be the first time he'd have the experience without Pat.

The night before the hunting trip with David, Clancy could hardly sleep. He felt nervous and sad and thought the whole idea might be a bad idea. Looking back, he remembered that all the "first time" events after Pat died—the first Christmas, the first birthday, the first Father's Day—were all hard, but nothing felt more difficult for him than that first hunting trip.

He went anyway. He got up the next morning, loaded his hunting gear in David's truck and took off. Just as he expected, it was really difficult and every footfall, every goose that flew, reminded him of his dad. But the trip, and being outdoors again, also felt good. The hunting trip ended up being healing as well, a way to reconnect with his dad's memory.

For the next several weeks, Clancy and David went hunting

several times a week. This person who had been almost a stranger prior to the accident became a good friend and important companion. I was so thankful for David and the caring he showed my son.

Still, I could never quite let go of the worry that a storm was coming.

Then, the other shoe fell. Just after Thanksgiving, one of my sisters-in-law said in passing, "I heard about Clancy being charged." I was stunned. I talked to Clancy and he said he hadn't heard anything. Surely it must be a misunderstanding or the DA's office would have notified him first. I called the county to enquire again. I was told that they might be trying to notify him with a certified letter. Still no real answers!

On November 29th, I got a call from a woman named Lois[1]. She said she was the Victim's Advocate for the Lincoln County district attorney and she had been assigned to support me as they charged the person who was responsible for the accident that had killed my husband. It took me a few moments even to grasp what she was saying. This was the first official news we had heard that Clancy was going to be charged and it didn't come to Clancy. He still hadn't been contacted; we'd received no information in the mail or by telephone. And yet this woman seemed to think she was doing me a favor, letting me know that the Lincoln County district attorney was going to seek "justice" for my husband's death, and that it was her job to help me take part. I couldn't tell if she was being malicious, insensitive, or was just incredibly dense.

"They're charging my son, Clancy?" I asked.

---

1 Not her real name.

"Yes," she said. I could hear her flipping through paperwork on the other end of the telephone line. "He's being charged with Careless Driving, Resulting in a Death."

"That's crazy!" I said. "He wasn't charged at the scene. He was driving under the speed limit. His dad wasn't wearing a seat belt." I tried to stop myself from shouting through the phone line. "My son lost his father. Isn't that enough?"

"That's not my call, Ma'am," she said. "I'm just letting you know that you have a right as the victim of this crime to be present at the arraignment hearing, which will be on January 3, 2011." She then told me that as the wife of the person killed, I was entitled to request reimbursement for the funeral expenses. If it were granted, the person charged would be required to pay it to the court. I asked her why in the world would I ask that the court require my innocent son to pay for his father's funeral? This woman delivered her information with no apologies for having to ask such a ridiculous, painful question. She seemed unable to grasp that the victim's wife was also the mother of the person being accused. I kept reminding her but she didn't care. She was the most insensitive, heartless person I'd ever spoken to, at least thus far in my life. Little did I know that she was not the last person I would encounter with this same heartless disposition.

Shaking, I hung up the phone. I immediately phoned my sister Barbara. I filled her in on the entire conversation, and then asked her if she would be the one to talk to this monster of a person if the need arose in the future. Barbara and I both agreed that we needed to find the best defense attorney in town. I scanned through the contact list on my phone until I came to one name—

Jack Woodward[2]—and hit "Dial."

I had known Jack for years. His daughter, Emily,[3] had been one of Sadie's best friends since kindergarten, and we had often seen him and Emily's mom at school events, or driving our daughters to each others' houses. In addition to being an attorney, Jack was also one of Colorado's Congressmen. A week or two after the accident, I had received a handwritten letter from Washington D.C. with the gold eagle crest on the top of the letterhead. In it were heart-felt words penned in royal blue ink. Jack expressed his deepest sympathies to us on Pat's death. He said that if there was anything he could do to help, please let him know. I decided to take him up on his offer. I hoped he might have some idea about who we could contact about this crazy situation.

Jack was frustrated by the development and said he would also make a few calls himself. In the meantime, he recommended that we hire a good attorney for Clancy. He stressed that it was important that we find someone with whom we felt comfortable, and recommended that we talk to a number of different people, but he gave us the name of three attorneys he had worked with in the past who did criminal defense. The top two on the list were brothers, Gary and Ken Kramer. He suggested I start with them.

At this point I was almost beside myself. I'd never talked to a lawyer professionally, and I wasn't sure what to ask. My sister Barbara, however, had worked with attorneys for years in many different capacities, so I asked her if she would mind calling to interview the attorneys. I gave her the names of the Kramers.

---

2 Not his real name.
3 Not her real name.

Barbara reached Ken Kramer first, who said that his brother Gary was probably the better choice for us as he worked more with criminal charges. He listened to the details of the case and said that he and his brother knew both the district attorney, a woman named Ceci Smith[4], as well as the deputy district attorney, a man named John Kendrick[5]. They'd had interactions with both people from the DA's office and said they seemed like reasonable people. He couldn't make any promises, of course, but it wasn't unlikely that they would be able to work out some sort of plea bargain. He promised to have Gary call back.

Gary called Barbara within an hour, listening carefully and asking a few more questions. He explained that the Careless Driving Resulting in a Death charge carried a potential one-year jail term, plus automatic revocation of the driver's license and a serious fine. It seemed crazy to think that they would actually work to put Clancy in jail, but he'd have to talk to the DA to find out what they were thinking. He also said he knew the chief of a Denver fire station and he would ask if a conviction would end Clancy's career options as a public servant, but his guess was that it was true. Like Ken, Gary said since he knew both the DA and the deputy DA and felt comfortable talking with them. He had no reason to believe that they would not be reasonable. No promises, of course.

Gary said that it seemed strange, however, that the district attorney was even pursuing the case. There didn't appear to be any extenuating circumstances—drug or alcohol use, reckless

---

4 Not her real name.
5 Not his real name.

behavior—that would lead them to make the charge. He wondered aloud if after the DA's office finished their investigation they had uncovered some incriminating fact that I was not aware of. Perhaps they found evidence that Clancy had been speeding or some other problem. Barbara assured him that both Josh and Clancy believed he had been driving under the speed limit. Gary said that they just couldn't know until they heard the DA's position.

He also stressed that if we were to hire him, Clancy would be his client, not any of the rest of us. Although he would try to be responsive to me and other family members, Clancy was the person whose opinion mattered most. He talked a lot about what Clancy must be going through at that point, and said he believed that Clancy needed time to grieve his father's death. He thought it would be best if the justice system would just leave him alone. If that wasn't going to happen, however, Clancy had to feel good about the decision to hire him. He recommended interviewing other attorneys, but said that he hoped that once he was able to talk to the DA's office, everything could be plea bargained and resolved quickly. There was even a chance it could be resolved before Christmas.

Barbara called me with the information. I felt that I could trust the recommendation of Jack Woodward. Barbara also felt comfortable with Gary and the types of questions he asked. I didn't want to waste any time. I called Gary Kramer's office and made an appointment for Clancy and me to meet with him the next day.

Getting to Know
Sadie

L ittle miss Sadie Kay is my second child. She is twenty-two months younger than her older brother Clancy. Given the closeness in age, I was lucky that she was such an easy baby. Being engulfed by the sea of brothers, she is strong, courageous, athletic and fluent in boy slang. She can hold her own in a family game of football. She can walk a slack line or ride a dirt bike.

She does all of these things, however, with a grace and beauty of her own. When she was just fourteen, Pat, Clancy, Sadie and I took an intensive three-day handgun-shooting course. On the last day the instructor had the whole class stop and watch her draw and shoot at the target. He pointed out the absolute fluidity of the way she performed. She wasn't the fastest or the most accurate shooter in the class, but she showed a presence and a poise that I marveled to see. And although she can at other times be something of a klutz, and has suffered more broken bones than her brothers, when she is focused on mastering a specific skill, she always shines.

She is also her father's daughter. As she gets older, more and more people think she and I have a strong family resemblance, but she is more like her dad. She is strikingly beautiful with one of her  dad's dimples. But she shares Pat's emotional characteristics along with the physical ones. She is very quiet and is never the one talking in a group. She listens and supports those whom she loves, and is the most loyal and steady friend. Sadie is athletic and competitive, and she must get that from her dad because I am not athletic at all and I hate competition. Sadie has a unparalleled drive and determination, just like Pat.

But Sadie also had assets and interests all her own. Sadie loves to dance. Dancing was this girl's passion from a very young age.

When Sadie was about three, my mom noticed a little dance studio near our house. Since Sadie was always twirling and jiving, my mom thought it was a good idea to enroll her in a beginner ballet class. When we signed her up they suggested that it was a good idea to do two one-hour classes a week so she'd progress more quickly. We would also get a big discount on the additional day. The first half hour of each class would be ballet and the second would be tap. Sadie was a natural and she loved it right away. It soon became the thing she looked forward to the most.

Not long after she started, my niece Elizabeth, Sadie's cousin, joined her. Elizabeth is six months older than Sadie

 and really the sister she always wanted. With our families living about four houses away from each other, Sadie and Elizabeth were inseparable. It was a good thing that they both loved to dance because they spent all of their time doing it. The two could practice what they were learning in class, together at home, or wherever we happened to be. Often it was in the grocery store or at church, or back and forth to each others houses. They didn't walk anywhere. They danced! This continued on through elementary school, middle school and high school where they were both on the dance team and were dancers in all the musicals. This love of dancing she didn't get from her father. At least we didn't think so.

Pat would not dance. Yes, sure, in the privacy of our own home after dinner he frequently moonwalked through the kitchen, but never at weddings or in public. Even at our high school prom he refused to dance, not even one slow dance.

When Pat started to realize how important this was to his only daughter, he began to think about the father-daughter dance at her wedding someday. Sadie had told him she expected him to participate in a choreographed dance with her. Pat wanted to be up for the job.

When Sadie was a senior in high school my niece Jaci (my sister Karla's daughter) got engaged and enrolled in a ballroom dancing class. She asked us if we would like to take the class also with Karla, my brother-in-law Andy, my parents, and some other family. This was our opportunity. Pat was somewhat reluctant but I was able to talk him into it. It was a blast! We discovered that we loved dancing together and Pat thought that by the time his little girl got married, he'd be able to dance adequately with her and not embarrass either one of them. We talked Sadie into attending a few classes as well so she could dance with her dad at Jaci's wedding.

Of course, Sadie picked up in a matter of minutes what had taken the rest of us hours upon hours to learn. But you should have seen Pat's face dancing with her. It was delightful! After that wedding, Pat and I continued taking lessons. We learned a few other styles of ballroom dancing and tried them out at other family weddings. Pat had heard "Cinderella," the song by Steven

Curtis Chapman' about dancing with his daughter, and Pat was sure he'd be ready when the time came for the dance with his own Cinderella. Sadie loved the song as well, and even though she was a long way from getting married—no boyfriend, no one waiting in the wings—she had figured out the father-daughter dance. It was the only part of any eventual wedding plan that she knew for sure.

I don't know if her poise and elegance was inherited or she gained it from a lot of years of dance. Maybe both. It doesn't really matter, I guess, where she got it. She didn't pursue dancing as a career option, but if you happen see her these days, she's still always dancing.

CHAPTER 11

HOMESICK

It was December in Denver, which means it was cold. I was driving home from work alone, listening to the radio. Most of the time, I couldn't handle the music. Music can hold so much emotion within it, and at times I felt I couldn't bear to hear it, as if my body couldn't handle the impact. Plus, so many songs reminded me of fun times I'd had with Pat. But this day I thought I'd try it again. Almost immediately, a song by the Christian group Mercy Me called "Homesick" came on. I'd heard it before, but had never really, REALLY thought about the words. This day I listened and felt a connection:

> *You're in a better place, I've heard a thousand times*
> *And at least a thousand times I've rejoiced for you.*
> *But the reason why I'm broken, the reason why I cry*
> *Is how long must I wait to be with you?*

If I close my eyes and I see your face,
If home's where my heart is, then I'm out of place.
Lord, won't you give me strength to
make it through somehow?
I've never been more homesick than now.

Help me, Lord, 'cause I don't understand your ways.
The reason why I wonder if I'll ever know.
But even if you showed me, the hurt would be the same
Cause I'm still here so far away from home.

This song captured what I was feeling exactly. It wasn't the initial shock or sadness. I wasn't spending hours on the floor of my bathroom anymore. To people watching me from a distance, I probably looked like I was doing fine. But what I felt was homesick for a place I wanted to be but wasn't. I felt disconnected, adrift. Like a wanderer in a foreign place, I couldn't figure out where home was.

In addition, I was strangely aware that the year was coming to an end. Pat had been alive in 2010, and I didn't want the calendar to roll over into 2011, which would be the first year he wouldn't see. I realized that part of grief is missing the life you had with the person you lost, missing the way he peeled a hard-boiled egg or laughed at a joke. But this grief was balanced with an equal fear of moving on and having any memories that did not include him. I was only fourteen years old when I first noticed him at church. He was the center of everything after that moment. I couldn't get my head around a different sort of life. I did not want to enter a year that he did not exist in. Is this not being able to let go?

Sadie turned 20 in early December and it was a bittersweet day. I was so proud of the lovely woman our daughter was becoming, but this birthday was also the first one for our family without Pat. It was a reminder that, unlike him, we would all continue to get older. Our lives would go on, whether we wanted them to or not, and we were being pushed into an unfamiliar future. I think we all wanted to hang on. Sadie didn't want to celebrate her birthday, and I think it was for this same reason. We didn't want a milestone with Pat not in it.

On the day of Sadie's birthday, Clancy wrote this post on Facebook, and I know he wrote what we were all thinking:

> *Missing Daddy lots . . . I miss the days when I would run out and give him a huge hug and kiss him on the cheek before I went to bed. All the funny conversations we had on the way to work everyday, the time we spent together out in the woods or laying on the freezing cold rock hard ground watching the pink sun come up over the horizon while we were goose hunting.*
>
> *I miss that funny grin he would always get when he did something mischievous, the way he laughed when I hit my thumb with a hammer or got hurt at work, but at the same time I knew just how much he cared about me and that he was concerned when he needed to be. I miss the way his smile could light up an entire room, how contagious his laugh was, and how passionate he was about everything in his life. I miss how he could look at you without even saying anything and you knew he was proud of you.*

I miss the way he would smile at me when he made a diving play in the outfield next to me and jumped up with a huge smile on his face. I miss the way we used to wrestle around the house and pretend to fight . . . Even when some of the punches accidentally made contact. I miss playing catch with him in the yard, and how he would come play with all the cousins at the family get-togethers. I miss singing next to him in the church ensemble, and how we would laugh at each other when we messed up. I miss our family dinners, even if it was the drive-through at Wendy's or Taco Bell occasionally.

And more than anything, I miss the time we spent together as a family—vacations, dinner, working on the house, the drives to church or skiing, the one time we got the whole family to go camping together, or even just sitting on the couch watching a movie all together. I guess I just miss my superman. I love you, Daddy.

We all missed Pat, of course. And we all woke up every morning, figuring out new ways to move forward. Part of the puzzle I faced that December was trying to get some resolution to Clancy's legal situation. I really missed having Pat by my side to support me, helping me to figure out what to do. I'd sometimes catch myself thinking, "If only Pat were here, this legal battle wouldn't be so hard." And then I'd realize that if Pat were here, we wouldn't be facing the legal battle.

And it was a battle. By the second week in December, Clancy had still not received a court summons. By that point, the only person we had talked to from Lincoln County was Lois, the Victim's Advocate who had been so insensitive the first time that

I decided never to talk to her again. I received a packet from her that gave me information about my Victim's Rights, stating that I would have a right to be at the trial and to make a statement about how the accused's crime had affected me. The thought of talking to her again made my skin crawl, but she seemed to be our only resource about what was happening. I called and left a message for her, asking if she could tell me where Clancy's paperwork was. I kept my phone nearby, waiting for the call, and every time the phone rang, my stomach lurched, wondering if it would be Lois.

She never called. Finally, three days later, my sister Barbara said she'd try to reach her. Strangely, Lois picked up the phone when Barbara called, but was completely uncooperative. Initially, she objected to giving Barbara any information at all, but eventually she said she'd heard that the Summons had been filed with the Court, sent out, but hadn't been returned. That was all the information she would be willing to share. Finally, Barbara explained that she understood this was an unusual situation for Lois, but that we would really like to find someone to help us. If Lois could not or would not be that person, did she know of anyone else who could?

"I'll give you this last piece of information," Lois told her, "and then I'm finished talking with you. Because the summons had been filed with the court, the court clerk might be able to send out another copy to Clancy. "The clerk probably won't talk to you either because you aren't related to Clancy"—apparently, being an aunt does not count—"but you can try."

Barbara called the court and finally got through to a helpful person. The clerk looked up the file and learned that the summons had listed the address for Clancy's apartment but had not included an apartment number. She took down the correct address and said she'd be happy to send Clancy a copy, and accepted that Barbara was a "close enough" relative to make this request on his behalf. She sent the copy to Clancy in the mail.

Nearly a month after we first heard that Clancy was going to be charged, he finally received the information in the mail. He was summoned to appear at a hearing in Hugo, Colorado, the county seat two hours from Denver, on January 3rd. We quickly signed the paperwork to hire Gary to represent Clancy in the hope that the situation could be resolved before Christmas. By then, however, it was already the third week in December, and when Gary tried to call the district attorney's office, he never received a return phone call. He surmised that everyone was already away for the holidays. The only information Gary heard was that they had pushed back Clancy's advisement hearing until January 11th because he hadn't had a chance to talk with the district attorney. Clancy would not appear before the judge. This would just be a conference with the DA. We would have to wait until then to learn anything more.

Waiting.

By this point, it felt like most of my life was about waiting. This was the season of Advent, the period of waiting before the celebration of Christ's birth. Normally, the month of December is a pleasant sort of waiting, anticipation for Christmas and family gatherings and gift giving and special church services. But this felt like a different sort of waiting for me. I was waiting for things to stop hurting so much. Waiting for things to stop going from bad to worse. Waiting for the season of Christmas carols and shopping and parties to be over. We were waiting for resolution for Clancy's legal situation. Waiting for the Wolff house to be finished so my family could move into a more permanent home. Waiting for the moment when I could again feel some sort of hope for the future. Waiting to feel like I belonged in my own life.

Waiting.

Waiting.

Waiting.

The refrain from the Mercy Me song came back to me.

And I close my eyes and I see your face.
If home's where my heart is then I'm out of place.
Lord, won't you give me strength to make it through somehow.
Won't you give me strength to make it through somehow.
Won't you give me strength to make it through somehow.

I've never been more homesick than now.

CHAPTER 12
CHRISTMAS EVE

It was Christmas Eve, an unusually warm, sunny day in Denver. I'd endured the wind-up toward the holiday. Early in the fall, before Pat's accident, we had talked about what we wanted to do for gifts for our families. Sadie, the chef in our family, had been experimenting with sea salt caramels and other treats, so we decided that we would give our families special food baskets. The basket would include caramels and apricot wine that my mom had made. We'd give jars of wild honey from the bee hives kept by my parents' neighbors. My parents' property included a stone quarry so we thought we'd cut slabs of sandstone that worked well as bread baking stones in the oven. We had it all planned out. In Pat's absence, my parents once again stepped in to help me put everything together, cutting the stone in sections and wrapping up the food. The baskets sat under the hastily set-up Christmas tree in our apartment, ready to be handed out the next day. I wasn't looking forward to Christmas, but it felt like this would be one last time Pat would participate in the holiday.

That night I was delivering some of the Christmas presents. I had a basket I wanted to take to Malcolm and his wife Judy. Normally, I disliked being alone. It wasn't that I needed to be talking all the time, but I found the presence of other people comforting. This afternoon, however, I was on my own, so I drove through the unusually deserted neighborhoods of Denver and let my thoughts go.

Since Pat died, I'd been looking for signs that things would be okay. I still wanted to believe in a miracle, and not just any miracle but the mother of all miracles. I wanted somehow for Pat's ashes, which at that time sat in a box on a shelf in Russ and Tracy's house, to be reassembled into my husband. Irrational or not, I wanted Pat to surprise me, to walk into our home, hands cold from shoveling snow, and stick them under my shirt on my bare stomach. I still had his cell phone and refused to cancel the contract because I wanted to be able to call his number and hear his voice asking me to leave a message. Sometimes I sent text messages to Pat and stood there, looking at the screen on my phone, waiting for some divine message to come to me from beyond. I wanted connection. I wanted reassurance. I wanted to feel grounded.

I also wanted some evidence that God was beside me. Although people frequently talked about feeling God's arms around them, I have to say it never felt that way to me. It was tempting to believe that my faith was somehow not firm enough to sense the presence of God in that way, but I came to believe that God's comfort comes to us in different, less tangible ways.

Looking back, I realized that there were brief moments when I felt some relief from my anxiety and grief, and I think that these were times when God was comforting me. Sometimes this comfort would just be for an hour, but I was really grateful for even an hour of comfort.

Still, on that Christmas Eve, I felt like I wanted something more.

I pulled onto the highway and settled into a steady speed. For some reason, I remembered a story I'd heard from my friend Corrie. In addition to being a member of our church, Corrie is an ICU Nurse at Children's Hospital, along with another friend, Lukas, who works as our church's worship leader. Often, Corrie worked the day shift while Lukas worked nights. I had run into her at church one day and asked how she was doing.

"I'm doing really well, actually," she said. "I just had an amazing week at work."

Intrigued, I asked her to tell me why.

Her story involved a family that was staying at a large ranch in the woods outside Durango, Colorado, a mountain town in the southwest corner of Colorado. The ranch was owned by a retired surgeon and his wife. They had invited all of their children and grandchildren for a visit and a large crowd was staying at their house. One evening, the parents were getting all the kids ready for bed. One mom, wrestling her 21-month-old son Gore into pajamas, realized that she was missing his pajama bottoms. She turned away for a moment to find them and to check on what his older brother and sister were doing. When she turned back to finish getting him ready for bed, Gore was gone.

Panicked, she ran for the door, still clutching the pajama bottoms. Gore had just learned to unlatch the screen door of the cabin, which was not far from an irrigation ditch filled with the icy cold snow runoff from the Colorado mountains. She looked along the length of the ditch but, not seeing him, ran back inside to see if he was playing with his siblings. He wasn't there.

The mother's calling alerted other family members who went into the woods and along the length of the ditch, searching for Gore. By then, it had been 25 minutes since he'd gone missing. Someone screamed from the back of the property. The mother suspected the worst.

"Call 9-1-1," she screamed, racing toward the sound. "It's going to be bad!"

She saw her cousin walking down the center of the ditch holding the unconscious body of her son. Still wearing his pajama top and diaper, Gore had been pinned under a log, facedown beneath the water. The cousin handed Gore to his grandfather, the retired surgeon, who immediately began CPR. Minutes passed with no heartbeat and no pulse. Family members traded off giving CPR until the ambulance arrived. As they watched the ambulance take off for a nearby hospital, they were sure Gore was dead.

Emergency workers continued to try to get Gore's little heart to start beating. They shocked him and would briefly get a rhythm, only to have it stop again. By the time he reached the hospital, he'd been unconscious, not breathing, and without a heartbeat for an hour. Then, somehow, the doctors were able to restart his heart and keep it stable. They told the family they were airlifting Gore to Children's Hospital in Denver where he could receive more treatment, but they warned the parents that given how long he'd been down, Gore was likely to be in a persistent vegetative state.

At Children's Hospital, the doctors gave Gore a less than a one percent chance of ever walking or talking again. He breathed with the support of a ventilator, and his robotic movements indicated brain damage. They decided to try an experimental treatment, lowering Gore's body temperature to 90 degrees and planned to keep it there for days in the hope it would give Gore's brain a chance to recover.

Gore was placed under Corrie and Lukas's care. Gore's room was kept cold, and the parents stayed by his side wearing coats and hats, even though it was July. Lukas and Corrie administered a paralytic medication to keep him still and stable. After a while, Lukas was instructed to reduce the paralytic drug, and he noticed Gore reaching to remove the intubation tube. He thought that this was more brain ability than a patient in a vegetative condition should have, and after conferring with Corrie, they suggested that Gore have a new CAT scan.

Corrie was present during the scan and watched the monitor the whole time. Although she was not formally trained to read the results, what she saw looked like normal brain activity to her, which completely thrilled and surprised her. After the scan, the doctors decided to warm Gore's body slowly. As they did, Gore just woke up, acting completely normal. His MRI showed no brain damage.

For Corrie, accustomed to seeing the most tragic outcomes in her line of work, this was indeed a welcomed story. She hadn't often seen such a miracle first-hand, and this did indeed qualify as a miracle. It just seemed impossible that a little boy could be without a pulse or oxygen for that long and come back completely whole. To Corrie, and to the rest of us, it seemed evidence of a loving, powerful God at work.

I encouraged both Corrie and Lukas to share the story with our church. And although I didn't know Gore's parents at the time, I later met them at a dinner at Corrie's house. Gore's mom told me that she was really struggling with why God had chosen to save Gore in such a miraculous way, but to then take Pat, a strong, capable man who offered so much to his family, his church and his community. It didn't seem right, somehow. Couldn't God have sent a miracle to save Pat as well?

This was the question that came to me in the quiet of my car on Christmas Eve. Why hadn't God chosen to give me a miracle and to save Pat. Although I believed from the first day Pat died that Pat's time had come and that God was in charge of both the timing and the outcome, this was the first time I really let myself ask the question this simple question: Why?

The more I thought about it, the crazier it seemed that the accident had had the power to kill Pat. Both Clancy and Josh had survived the accident relatively unhurt. But so many little things had to go wrong for Pat to die in the same incident. First of all was the fact that he had been so determined to take Clancy on the trip. Had he just gone with Josh, he probably would have driven and would have been in the front seat with his seat belt fastened. Pat had been to that location before, unlike Clancy, and had an amazing memory of where he had driven. As it was, he was crammed in the back and either hadn't fastened his seatbelt at all, or had just not refastened it after getting back in the truck at the gas station. The reconstruction of the accident itself, based from the skid marks and the investigation of the scene, indicated that the truck rolled only half a turn, landing on its top, but no one could figure out how Pat could have been thrown from the small back window of the cab and still landed underneath the truck. Furthermore, not all of his body was pinned, just a small corner of his chest over his heart. And, Pat wasn't by himself; Clancy and Josh, two of the strongest men I know, were with him, and try as they might, could not budge the truck or wiggle Pat out from beneath it. Pat himself was so physically strong. No one could lift more, carry more, run faster or farther, than Pat. If anyone should have been able to survive an accident, or hang on until help arrived, it was Pat. He stayed alive for about thirty minutes while being pinned by the truck, but he stopped breathing only three minutes before the ambulance arrived. Three minutes! Why couldn't the paramedics revive him after three minutes, when Gore came back after being down for an hour?

I thought about the unlikelihood that Pat had died, compared with the unlikelihood that Gore survived. And then I had this thought: We love to say that when something unexpected happens and it's good, it's a miracle and evidence of God's love and power. But when something unexpected happens and it's bad, we call it a tragedy. But it's the same amount of God in both events. I may struggle with the consequences of Pat's death, which are very real and very, very hard. But in the quiet of my car on my Christmas Eve drive, God revealed to me that Pat's death was just as much a miracle. A tragic miracle, to be sure. But there still might be something lovely about it. There was a perfect timing to Gore's recovery, and a perfect timing to Pat's death.

Suddenly, I remembered the familiar passage from Ecclesiastes 3 and saw it with fresh eyes:

> *For everything there is a season and a time for every matter under heaven; a time to be born, and a time to die; a time to plant, and a time to pluck up what is planted; a time to kill and a time to heal; a time to break down, and a time to build up; a time to weep and a time to laugh; a time to mourn and a time to dance; a time to cast away stones, and a time to gather stones together; a time to embrace, and a time to refrain from embracing; a time to seek, and a time to lose; a time to keep, and a time to cast away; a time to tear, and a time to sew; a time to keep silent, and a time to speak; a time to love, and a time to hate; a time for war, and a time for peace.*

I finally got to a place where I could think—and really understand in a place deeper than mere thinking—that God's perfect timing was at work in my life and in the lives of my children. What was the significance of the timing, that it took twenty-four years of being married to Pat to build our family and raise our children in a way that God could use them? What would it mean that Clancy had 21 years with his Dad, Sadie 19 years, Jesse, 16 years, and James 13? What was God hoping to do through them? How amazing to think that not only were Pat's days numbered before the beginning of time, but his exact days with each child were perfectly designed to make them who they are.

Each one of the four kids had the best of Pat's moments independent of each other. Pat held James every single night from after dinner until bed time. Pat had coached his baseball team for several years. They had many rides to practice and games together. Jesse did many car repairs with Pat and enjoyed many weekend projects. He loved to complete a job and didn't tire even after a long day as long as he was at his dad's side. Sadie, in the five weeks before the accident, had been coming home from her early morning labs in culinary school and making Pat lunch and eating it with her. Pat was not always sure how to communicate with a daughter, but she was the only girl and he had an obvious soft spot for her. Clancy as the oldest got the most time with him of all the kids. He was working with him building houses. They played together on a men's softball team, and Pat passed down to him his obsession with hunting. It was amazing to think that all of these details were designed. It all had significance. I didn't really think at the time about how God could be using me in all of this, but it was comforting to think that there was some promise for my children. Maybe there would be a way to look at the future.

For the first time since October 6th, I felt some comfort. It didn't come to me in a booming voice from heaven. I didn't actually feel God's arms wrapped around me. But in the quiet of my car I found a form of peace.

I finished my errands and went home. I didn't share my thoughts with anyone at the time, but they comforted me through the evening. We woke the next morning to our first Christmas without Pat. Truly, I would have preferred to skip the day altogether, but it appeared that Christmas showed up whether we liked it or not. We'd made plans to spend it with the McKendry's at Pat's parents' house, and it was a quiet, solemn day. Everyone was a little bit sad. Still, it didn't carry the same despair I felt at Thanksgiving, just a month before. I was a little bit buoyed by my Christmas Eve revelations, and began to allow myself to feel hopeful that I could eventually find some joy and happiness again. I still didn't feel it. I still didn't even really know how it was possible, but I had a new faith that it could happen. I recalled the passage from Philippians chapter 3: "But one thing I do: Forgetting what is behind and straining toward what is ahead, I press on toward the goal to win the prize for which God has called me heavenward in Christ Jesus."

At one point, Russ came and sat next to me on the couch, handing me a glass of wine.

"You seem good today," he said. "What's different."

And so I told him about my car ride. I told him about miracles. And I told him about hope. Which I guess is about as good a Christmas gift as any.

CHAPTER 13

JUSTICE

I spent New Year's Eve at Russ and Tracy's house with several members of their family. I waited for the minutes to tick away until the arrival of the New Year, and then gathered my kids and we made our way back to our apartment. I crawled into bed but felt unable to sleep, swarmed by the ever-present thoughts in my head.

My sister Barbara had given me a journal for Christmas. She had encouraged me to write about what I was going through and sent along a black, leather-bound Moleskine notebook and a black felt-tipped pen. I pulled both of them out in those early hours of New Year's Day, 2011, and tried to write something down.

January 1, 2011

As everyone is wishing a happy new year on Facebook, I'm alone in my bed for the first time in 29 years. I keep thinking that I have the same difficult struggles ahead that were there 30 minutes ago. Sadness fell over me in the last hours of 2010 as I realized that we mark a person's life by the year that they were born and the year they die. Pat's years were 1965 and 2010 and both have passed now. I am mostly returning to the disbelief that has been my state of mind for much of the last three months. How did this happen? Is this really my life and not some poor family that I have heard about in passing? God, I must trust you! I would certainly not have picked this path to walk. I long to walk the streets of gold and not measure time by days and years. Tonight I beg God for mercy and grace.

We are all having to figure out how to live each new moment.

Living each new moment. How does one actually go about doing that? This was the first full year in which I would live without Pat, and I knew I would only be able to do it a moment at a time. But there were still big issues looming in front of us.

The scariest thing still before us was Clancy's legal battle. It was hard enough to imagine how my children were managing their lives with the loss of their father. It was another level of grief altogether realizing that the justice system wanted to somehow blame my son for Pat's death. With the reassurances from Gary, Clancy's attorney, we'd been able to push back some of the worry long enough to get us through the holidays, but once the calendar rolled into January, Clancy's impending hearing once again took top priority on my list of concerns.

January 11, 2011, was a Tuesday. The hearing was set for eleven o'clock in Hugo, Colorado, the Lincoln County seat. Because it was a two hour drive from Denver, Clancy and I left at eight thirty, planning to arrive early in order to have thirty minutes to meet with Gary, Clancy's attorney, before the actual hearing. I took the day off of work and rode along with Clancy with high hopes for a resolution and an acceptable outcome. He appeared a bit nervous, but seemed to be handling the stress well. He was dressed in a pastel lavender button up dress shirt and grey pinstriped trousers, and I was pleased with his selection. He was clean shaven and his cousin Elizabeth had given him a haircut the night before. He looked like an intelligent, thoughtful young man.

We met Gary at the courthouse. We asked if we could use an empty conference room to talk until we were called. The three of us sat in a plain white room with Gary on one side of a cheap, fake wood table and Clancy next to me facing him. Because Gary had not even had a chance to discuss Clancy's case with anyone from the district attorney's office prior to this day, the hearing would not be before a judge. Instead, we would be meeting with John Kendrick, the deputy district attorney. John was someone Gary had worked with before, and although we were nervous to be in the courtroom at all, we hoped we might receive some positive news. More than anything, I wanted the accident to be behind us—behind Clancy, especially—so that we could all move forward.

After waiting for what seemed like an eternity, we were finally called in to see Mr. Kendrick, who led us to his office that held a large desk nearly as big as the small room it was in. In front of the desk they had managed to squeeze two metal and vinyl chairs. Gary found another chair and pulled it into the doorway so he'd have a place to sit. Gary shook Kendrick's hand as we all took our seats. I immediately thought it seemed strange that Kendrick never addressed Clancy or me. We settled down in our chairs as the deputy D.A. opened a manila file and spread out some papers on the desk. Gary took out a legal pad and a pen and placed it in front of him, waiting to take notes.

A disturbing feeling came over the room. There was something strange about our interaction with Kendrick even before he said a word. Maybe that was part of the problem. Usually, when someone, even a stranger, hears that Pat had been killed in a car accident, they usually say something acknowledging our situation. "Sorry for your loss," or "That's terrible. How are you doing?" From Kendrick, however, we got nothing. I thought it seemed odd that he wouldn't look Clancy or me in the eye. He didn't address any of his comments to either of us. He asked no questions nor said anything to acknowledge the fact that my husband, Clancy's father, had died. It suddenly became hard to breathe.

My fears were not relieved when he started to speak directly to Gary. Gary asked Kendrick a few questions, trying to figure out what the district attorney's approach would be. Would Mr. Kendrick be open to a negotiation to reduce the charges? Perhaps drop them altogether?

Kendrick interrupted Gary mid-sentence.

"There will be no plea bargain," he said, scowling at Gary. "This is serious. Someone died."

I couldn't believe what I was hearing. I wanted to scream at this man. Did he think we didn't know that someone had died? Did he think I didn't notice that my husband was gone from my house, my bed, my life? Did he think my kids didn't understand the significance of the fact that there was now a gaping empty place which had once been filled with a man who would toss them a baseball, sit next to them in church, wrestle with them in the yard, or help them fix a truck engine? Could this man really think that anyone, anywhere, had any greater understanding of the seriousness of the situation? My heart beat loudly in my chest. I could feel Clancy stiffening next to me. I put my hand on his knee and squeezed tightly. I whispered to him, "You didn't do anything wrong." This was my precious son, and I felt fear for the first time that I might not be able to do enough to protect him.

The meeting got worse. It didn't appear that Kendrick had any specific information that would lead him to believe that Clancy had been driving carelessly or recklessly. He didn't produce evidence of speeding or improper behavior. The only thing he shared was that he himself had driven to the accident site that morning before our meeting (in full daylight, hours after the actual time of the accident) and he believed that Clancy should have been able to navigate the corner. Kendrick didn't know that it had never been Clancy's intention to turn at all, that he had thought he would just continue driving straight ahead until the road seemed to disappear in front of him. Gary didn't correct him on this point because he didn't want to tip off the DA's office about his potential trial strategy.

Gary reminded Kendrick that it had been dark at the time of the accident and that it would have been hard to see. Kendrick was unswayed and unresponsive. Gary asked if the DA's office would consider a deferred judgment, a plea bargain in which the DA's office would defer entering a conviction on Clancy's record until after an agreed-upon probationary period had been successfully completed.

"No way," said Kendrick. "That option is not on the table." The position the district attorney appeared to be taking was that because someone had died, they would seek to find someone to blame and punish. The only concession Kendrick was willing to make was that should Clancy plead guilty, he would consider asking the judge not to impose the maximum one year jail term, a consequence Clancy had been unaware was even a possibility until that day. There were no other options. Clancy could either plead guilty right away, or he could choose to have his guilt determined in a criminal trial. Gary took a deep breath and switched gears.

"In the event of a trial," he said, "I'm assuming that Josh Bard would be called to testify."

"That's right," said Kendrick.

"Since Josh is a professional baseball player, and the trial would most likely take place during baseball season, I'm wondering if you would agree to have Mr. Bard testify by deposition, as it is unlikely that he would be released from his schedule to appear in person."

"We will make no special concessions," said Kendrick. "As I've said, this is serious."

Gary told him that we needed time to think about our options and asked if we could schedule another meeting for the following month. We settled on a date in early February.

Stunned, we left the courthouse with Gary and went to a diner for lunch where we could discuss what had just happened. The more we talked over lunch with Gary, however, the more scared I felt. Gary didn't understand why the DA's office was pursuing this so aggressively, and agreed that it didn't really make sense. There was no "smoking gun," no obvious proof that Clancy had acted negligently. Something else was going on, and we had no idea what it was.

Since Clancy could not in good conscious plead guilty, we next discussed what would be involved should we have to go to trial. It wasn't good. Gary estimated that a trial would cost between $70,000 and $100,000. This was money I obviously didn't have. Some of these charges would include hiring a team to do our own accident reconstruction to counter anything the district attorney's office had conducted. We would also need to hire our own private investigator to talk to witnesses, people who lived in the area, or anyone else who had had a negative experience at the accident site.

In addition, we talked about the options for arranging a potential trial to minimize the impact on Josh. During the baseball season, it wouldn't be unusual for him to have games five or six days a week at any place across the country. Gary would, of course, try to get Josh's testimony scheduled for a day he had off, but he couldn't guarantee it. We knew that Josh would do whatever it took to help Clancy through this process. Still, we knew that asking Josh to appear in court during his professional season could cost him his career.

Clancy was more frustrated than I had ever seen him. This meeting had been a shock on several levels. First, he truly believed in his heart that he had done nothing wrong, and he was angry that anyone was trying to tell him that he should be punished for something he didn't do. He was so convinced of his innocence that it was hard for him to fathom that the justice system itself wouldn't protect him.

At the same time, however, he was shocked by this early experience of seeing how the system actually worked. For years, he had been planning to join the criminal justice system. He believed that there was a need in the world for people seeking justice, and for officials who could help see that justice was actually served. He wanted to help make that happen. He had kept his nose clean, and taken all the introductory criminal justice classes in college. He'd been planning to begin additional training later that same month, which he now had to put on hold until he could get these legal charges cleared up. It seemed strange that the system didn't seem to protect him.

In some ways, I felt grateful that he had no doubts at all about his innocence because I think it insulated him somewhat from the blame that the system was trying to assign. He was primarily frustrated that he had to respond to a charge that was unjust. He couldn't really believe, at that point anyway, that his innocence wouldn't be acknowledged.

I was also comforted that Josh, the only other witness to the accident, believed in Clancy's innocence as well. Josh kept telling me and Clancy that he saw the same thing Clancy saw that morning and would have done the exact same thing Clancy did. He told me in the front yard of the Wolff house the morning after the accident that he'd go to his grave making sure Clancy understood that.

At Gary's suggestion, we hired a re-enactment expert to visit the site to investigate the accident. The expert took with him the information from the accident report and said that he believed that everything was consistent with Clancy's account of the accident. He calculated that Clancy had been driving 45 miles per hour in a

55 mile per hour zone, and that after taking the corner, the truck had tipped onto the driver's side and rolled onto its roof, a 180-degree turn. He couldn't figure out how Pat had ended up underneath the corner of the upside-down truck cab.

The investigator also looked at the corner. There was a sign before the corner showing a curve ahead, but it was well off to the side of the road and in a ditch. It might have been hard to see, and it didn't list a recommended reduced speed. We had learned that one month prior to Pat's accident, a young woman, on her way to see her fiancé late in the evening, crashed in the same spot. She had never been there before and the corner caught her off guard, just as it had Clancy. From there the investigator interviewed the people living in the house near the corner and who had responded to the accident that morning. The woman said that there had been plenty of accidents on that corner, and people often go off the road. They had been asked several times to help people pull their cars out of the ditch and back on the road.

"We just never saw one this serious before," she said.

CHAPTER 14

THE WOLFF HOUSE

Even as we were trying to sort out and end Clancy's legal troubles, we were facing another issue: where to live. Friends had graciously paid for the six-month lease on my apartment, but it would expire soon and I needed to make a longer-term plan for where my family would live. I was surer than ever that I wanted to finish remodeling the Wolff house, sell it, and move into something that was easier for me to manage. Although I still had three children living at home with me, I knew I didn't have the long-term energy for extensive yard work and house maintenance.

I started looking around for options. I could move out of Denver, back into the suburbs near where we had lived for fifteen years, but I felt strongly that I wanted to continue to live near Russ and Tracy. In addition to having nearby support and back-up in a place that was a reasonable distance from the kids' schools, it felt like I was able to go back to something familiar. We had lived near

Russ and Tracy for so much of our lives it felt natural and comfortable to have that again.

Russ had already encouraged me to walk through some properties in the building where he and Tracy lived. Although they lived in a condo in a high-rise, there were a couple of townhouses at the base of the building on the street level that were for sale. They were both brick townhouses near a city park. One had three bedrooms that could accommodate my large family, and it was brand new. Plus, maintenance was handled by the condo organization. I had toured them in November, shortly after moving into the apartment.

Back then, I had walked through the townhouse with Tracy and the sales person for the complex, a woman named Terry. We went from room to room with Terry pointing out the lovely features of the place—the nearness of the park, the tall windows, the enclosed patio. I tried to be pleasant—really, I did—but I couldn't help but see it through Pat's eyes, with the perspective of a master builder. This was supposed to be one of the better townhouses in Denver, but all I saw were the cracks in the bathroom floor, the flaws in the baseboard, the bad job made of the painting. I suppose I communicated my negative attitude as I walked around because I overheard Tracy murmuring to Terry, "She's just lost her husband who was a custom builder. This is hard for her."

Plus, it was too expensive. It would take everything I earned from the sale of the Wolff house plus the entire amount in Pat's life insurance to be able to afford it. I thanked Terry for her time, but told her I didn't see any way it would work, no matter how nice the townhouse was, or how close it was to Russ and Tracy.

Terry understood, and I truly felt she wanted to help. She told me that she'd heard there might be a reduction in the price, and that it would be significant. If that happened, she would be sure to drop me an email.

I forgot about the townhouse and instead focused on getting the Wolff house ready to sell. And by that, I mean that I helped the horde of people who had come out to get the Wolff house ready to sell.

Work had started on the house almost as soon as I decided to sell it and we'd moved out. It was a huge project that would have been a job for any builder, including Pat. Even before we closed on the house, Pat had spent a week of his own time and our own money shoring up the foundation to get the building to the point where it would even pass an inspection and be ready for appraisal. Pat and I had big plans for the property, practically rebuilding it from the ground up. Sadie and I had started a blog called "From Lathe to Luster," and we looked forward to chronicling the developments of making this falling-down Victorian house into the gem we knew it could be.

Now, it was a different story. Gone were the grand schemes, replaced by plans to make the house and its existing floor plan livable and appealing. This mostly involved remodeling the kitchen and upgrading the house's only bathroom. It also meant refinishing, polishing, or repainting all of the surfaces—walls, floors, windows, and hardware. Although it wouldn't be a huge remodel in the way we had imagined, there was still no inch of the entire house that would remain untouched.

This involved a lot of work from a lot of people. Looking

back now, I am humbled and awed by the outpouring of support that came together to make the remodel happen.

Not surprisingly, the work started with my parents. Shortly after I had decided to sell the house and had settled into the new apartment, my father started doing all the demolition necessary to get the property ready for any contractors who would come in. Almost daily, he and my mother would drive to Denver. Sometimes, my mom would join him working at the house. Most of the time, he would first drop my mom off at our apartment where she would help with everything from housework to homework before heading over to the Wolff house by himself. He tore out what remained of the kitchen cabinets and fixtures, ripped up flooring, pulled down non-structural walls. He removed antique hinges and doorknobs and hardware. He pulled out floorboards and walls to expose the plumbing and electrical work. Although he himself wasn't a licensed contractor, he was a planner (who had built his own house from the ground up), and wanted to make sure that when the contractors who had volunteered their expertise and their crews to help us arrived at the site, they wouldn't be wasting their time. My dad served as the point person who helped coordinate all the volunteers, picked up supplies when they ran low, and picked up a hammer to help anyone who needed it. He did this five or six days a week, every week, for months.

Steve McKendry, Pat's brother and his construction partner for 25 years, stepped in as well. Despite dealing with an injured back and the demands of his own construction business, he took whatever time he needed to be at the house to help. He, like Pat, had the knowledge and experience to make things work. Steve took over the responsibility for all the challenging jobs that come with trying to make an old house new. He was largely responsible for remodeling the kitchen, preparing for and installing all new cabinets, making irregular floors and walls square, and making sure everything came together. We decided to renovate the enclosed front porch, and Steve took charge, directing the process to rip out the walls and replace them with posts and balusters. Steve and my dad worked closely together.

A large crowd of talented people joined them. Several contractors had volunteered their help free of charge. An electrician spent countless hours rewiring a jumbled-up, hazardous mess. A

plumbing contractor and a crew (whose salaries I assume he paid for) came in and replaced all the pipes in the entire house to get it up to code, as well as the furnace and hot water heater. A painter from our church offered to paint the exterior of the house. He provided the crew and the paint, and transformed the ugly pink stucco with a soft off-white color.

Dave McKendry, Pat's brother, is an accomplished interior painter and faux finisher. Dave brought over his own crew, including our nephew Casey, to repair and refinish all the walls and floors of the remainder of the house. He patched sheetrock and painted rooms. He refinished and painted the original oak floors in the main rooms. The stairs received a special faux finish. All of this was on his own time and with his own money. Pat's sister

Shell assisted Dave most Saturdays with paint and texture, and my friend Melissa could be found often in a back room working away with the most pleasant disposition.

There were so, so many others who came and helped. Each week I would post a notice on my Facebook page, letting people know that we were having a work party that weekend. Each Saturday, the kids and I would get up, grab coffee at Starbucks, and head over to the house, where we would be joined by Pat's sister and brothers and their families, my parents, aunt and uncle, and friends

from the church. One of my friends from work, along with his father-in-law, took on remodeling the only existing bathroom. People polished doorknobs and stripped paint from hardware. The storm windows were completely disassembled, cleaned, and put back together. My mom shopped for (and paid for) all new appliances. Some people pulled out and replaced the bathroom fixtures, while others laid and grouted new tile on walls and floors. Crews hung new cabinets on freshly finished walls. And through it all, more and more people arrived with food and drinks to nourish our building crew.

These were bittersweet moments for me. It brought back so many memories for me and my children of family time spent doing exactly this—remodeling a house. There were so many times when in the bustling activity we'd look around and expect to see Pat in the middle of it. In a way, it felt like we got to spend some time with him, or at least with his memory. This felt as familiar to us as anything, and it was still quality family time together just like old times, being goofy and laughing while we worked.

Of course, this also made it hard. It would be so tempting to believe that Pat was just up on a ladder somewhere, or at the hardware store picking up supplies. One day, Sadie and I were sitting next to each other on the floor trying to re-assemble an ornate doorknob. There had been laughter and sparring going on all day. She said to me exactly what I had been thinking, that we were "just one person short of the best time spent with family." Oh, how we missed him on those days.

It was, however, amazing to see the crowd of support that came together, and to see the Wolff house nearing completion. At the time, I still had a diminished ability to understand or even feel true joy, but even then I understood what an amazing gift this type of service was to me, to my children, and to Pat's memory. People came alongside me to help me do what I could not do myself, but which needed to be done nevertheless. Slowly, I let go of the image of what Pat and I thought the house would be, and instead allowed myself to see it being built for someone else's family. And it was turning out to be beautiful. The stainless steel appliances in the kitchen gleamed against the dark wood cabinets. The stately trim in all the rooms was set off with new coats of paint. The windows sparkled and the antique radiators steamed with comforting heat. It was absolutely lovely. The house that, for me, would have always represented tragedy and the loss of a dream, would be a beautiful home for another family. We listed it for sale. I wasn't expecting to make a profit on the house; I mostly wanted to get out of it the money Pat and I had invested. Because of the generosity of everyone who had donated the time, materials and cash to finish the remodel, the house was an incredible value. I just hoped that it would sell quickly in a recessed market.

Fortunately, it sold almost right away. We had a contract on the house to sell for the asking price, contingent upon our being able to finish the renovations on the house by the closing date, set for mid-March. A young couple made the offer and this would

be their first house. The wife had a sibling that lived nearby. This was a family eager to move into the Wolff house and make a fresh start.

My family needed a different kind of fresh start, and it came, not surprisingly, shortly after the New Year.

I was at work one day when I opened an email from Terry, the sales person from Russ and Tracy's complex. She told me that they had just lowered the price of the three-bedroom townhouse I had seen. Was I still looking? She listed the new asking price, and I was stunned. It was a significant reduction, now just within my financial range.

I quickly called Ally, the realtor I had used to buy and to sell the Wolff house. What did she think? Was this a crazy idea? Was it a good deal? Ally thought the townhouse was a good investment, especially at the reduced price. Still, she knew that it felt like a stretch and a significant financial commitment to me.

I talked to everyone I knew. I asked my parents. I worked through a budget with Russ. I talked with Josh and Lindsey. I called my sister and brother-in-law in Oregon to get their advice. I talked to Malcolm, my boss of almost thirty years. Everyone was cautious and careful, but seemed to think it could be a good opportunity.

I also prayed about it. I wanted to make a responsible decision. I was a widowed mother of four in a less than optimal financial situation. I didn't want to make a foolish decision that would jeopardize my future security. And yet I knew in my heart that we all needed the security a home could provide. But was this the right home? I asked God to make it apparent what I should do.

I decided to make a low offer, undercutting their reduced price and adding all sorts of contingencies. I asked them to replace the cracked tile I'd seen in the bathroom. I asked for a second parking space in the garage. I made the offer contingent on my getting financing, on the sale of the Wolff house, and on the closing being on the same day. I hoped that the sellers would use any one of these contingencies as a negotiating tool.

I was driving James home from school the next day, when I got a phone call from Ally.

"You won't believe this," she said.

"Oh dear," I thought, "What now?"

"They accepted your offer as is, Karyl." Ally laughed. "I've never seen anything like it. They even said you could pick out different tile for the bathrooms if you'd like."

"Seriously?" I felt an odd feeling in my chest that surprised me. After a few moments, I decided that it was a glimmer of hope. I'd become unaccustomed to the feeling.

Ally chuckled. "It feels like this was supposed to happen for some reason. It's got to be a 'God-thing.'"

A God-thing. Indeed.

Later in January, I had another dream about Pat. It was the first dream I'd had that wasn't scary or frustrating. We were in a tropical setting as if we were on vacation with the kids. We were next to a sparkling blue pool, surrounded by grass huts and palm trees. I sat on a lounge chair and looked up to see the kids playing in the water. Then I noticed that Pat was in the pool with them. We all knew that Pat had died and that he was gone, and we didn't know how or why he was able to be with us. We didn't care. I got up from my chair and went to him. I kissed him and wrapped my arms around him.

And then I woke up. Usually, this is the hardest moment of my day, when I realize that he is gone and won't ever be coming back. But this time was different. This time, I felt like I had actually been able to spend a brief moment with him, and it felt really nice to see him, even if it hadn't been "real."

I wrote a quick Facebook post:

"Nice to see you, honey, even if only in my dreams!"

CHAPTER 15
CLANCY TURNS 22

We started preparations for moving into our new home. Clancy was the only one of my children who would not be moving with us. Pat's accident and death had caught him at a strange crossroads in his life, that place between being a dependent member of our original family and setting out to create a life of his own. He had already started that process, moving into his own apartment, which was originally shared with a roommate and then taken on by himself. It was a small two-bedroom place furnished with pieces we'd given him from our house, or things picked up at Hobby Lobby. He was making decisions about the career he wanted and planning how to fit college in around working with his dad remodeling our house. It wasn't a complicated plan, or a complete one, but it was a plan.

And then there was the accident. Big plans were placed on hold. Even small things were no longer taken for granted. He hadn't been able to sleep since the accident. He'd always been a bit of an insomniac, but now he just couldn't seem to fall asleep—or stay asleep—in silence. Sleeping by himself in his quiet bedroom in an empty apartment became impossible. He took to falling asleep on the love seat in his living room in front of the television, which he left on all night. The love seat was a good three feet shorter than his 6 foot 3 inch frame, so he had chronic neck and back pain.

The court hearing early in January did nothing to encourage his dream of being in law enforcement. He felt disillusioned about the system's ability to fight for and win justice. If it was failing him, was it the right field for him to pursue as a career? He still liked the idea of protective services. He was drawn to working out in the field in a physically challenging environment. His reaction after living through his own accident reinforced for him that he would be capable of thinking clearly in emergency situations. He would still be able to work in public service in challenging, emergency situations. He started thinking that firefighting might be a better fit for him.

All of which would still become impossible if he ended up with a criminal charge on his record. To drive any sort of emergency vehicle—police car, fire truck, or ambulance—he'd have to have a clean record. There was so much at stake. Still, maybe there would be ways for him to get some training toward the goal of being a firefighter, even while waiting for his legal situation to clear up.

He learned that there was an EMT program being offered at Red Rocks Community College, which was fairly close to his apartment. My mother took him to enroll for the program and learned that it had already filled. Clancy felt defeated and frustrated that nothing seemed to be going his way. They asked if there was any way he could be added to the class as an overload and were told that they'd have to talk to the person in charge at the fire station in Arvada. The station was a few blocks from Clancy's apartment, so they drove over right away.

The person was not available when they arrived, so they wandered around the lobby of the station, waiting. My mom happened to notice a flyer on a bulletin board, advertising a different firefighter-training program that would be offered on site at the fire station itself. It was scheduled to begin in about two weeks. She pointed out the flyer to Clancy, who was very excited about the program. They finally got in to see the person in charge, who told them that both the EMT class and the training program mentioned on the flyer were closed. However, after hearing Clancy's story, he agreed to enroll Clancy in the firefighter-training program.

Clancy signed up that day. He was outfitted with his bunker gear and sent me a photo he'd taken with his cell phone of himself all decked out. I took in the yellow helmet, the immense coat and all the reflective tape. His mouth was covered but I could tell he was happy. This felt good to him, and I was grateful. Maybe things were going to work out for Clancy. Maybe, just

maybe, there would be a way through all of this mess and he could finally look forward to something good. He would be turning 22 in just a few days, and although I was concerned about how he would feel on his first birthday without his dad, I was pleased that things seemed to be going well, at least for a while.

And then, just as quickly, my hopes were dashed. The kids and I, minus Clancy, had gone out to dinner with Russ and Tracy. We were sitting in a loud restaurant when I started getting phone calls from people at my work. I knew I couldn't talk or hear in such a loud space so I didn't take the calls. Finally, after the fifth or sixth call, I started to wonder what was going on. When the next call came from Kathy Timmons, who works in our lab, I answered.

"Karyl, you've got to turn on the television," she said. "They're doing a piece about Clancy, and it doesn't look good."

She told me that she'd been watching American Idol when it went to a commercial break. The screen had gone black and was then filled with a full-screen picture of Pat's face, followed by a full-screen image of Clancy's senior photo. The news anchor broke in, saying they had a story about "young Clancy McKendry, a local man being charged for killing his father. The story tonight at 10!"

I felt completely blind-sided, angry and overwhelmed. Seriously! Couldn't they just leave us alone?

I could no longer face eating dinner. I tossed my wallet to the kids so they could pay for our food and took my phone outside to a quieter place. No one from the news station had contacted me or Clancy to ask permission or to find out how we felt about the situation. Russ, who had come out on the sidewalk to join me, said that someone from Fox news had called the church and spoke with Russ's assistant. Russ told them we were not interested in a story. Even if someone had managed to contact me I would have told them that we absolutely didn't want to have any story done, that I thought it was incredibly insensitive for my son to have his high school picture spread across the news media along with the implication that he'd killed his dad.

On top of that, I was even more concerned that if the district attorney, Ceci Smith, saw it, she might assume that we had something to do with it, and I was afraid it would be like throwing gasoline onto a fire. Things were bad and scary enough as it was. Why, oh why, did anyone feel like this was news! It was as traumatizing a moment as I had felt since the day I got the call that Pat had died.

I called Clancy's attorney to ask for his advice. I got Gary's voicemail and left a message. I paced the sidewalk until everyone finished dinner, then we all walked home. It was at times like these that I really missed Pat. I so much wanted to have him with me so we could just hash out this problem and figure out what to do.

Gary eventually called me back. He told me not to watch the news program. He felt it would just be too difficult to see. Instead, he would watch it and call me afterward and we could talk.

We went home and tried to calm down. The kids turned on the television, curious to see what the newscasters would say. I really didn't want to see the program. I put the dogs on their leashes and took them out for a walk. My plan was to be nowhere near a television during the broadcast. I walked around the block once, then twice, then a third time. When I felt it would be safe, I went back to the apartment.

I walked through the door, unbuttoning my coat, and just at that moment the segment about Clancy and Pat came on the news. I stood there by the doorway with my coat on and watched it. It wasn't as bad as I'd feared, as it was mostly a rehash of the news story the station ran right after the accident. I was most upset that it included an inaccurate graphic that attempted to re-enact the accident, showing the truck veering (the wrong way) around the corner, and implying that the truck rolled several times. To a casual viewer who knew nothing about the circumstances or the site, it made it look like Clancy was driving erratically. It made him look guilty, right there on a public television station, broadcast to hundreds of thousands of people. The news anchor, a dark-haired woman in a smart suit, shared the fact that Clancy had been charged with Careless Driving Resulting in Death. Fortunately, she stated that the station hadn't been able to reach the family for a comment, and ended by saying, "as if the family hasn't suffered enough."

Gary called a few minutes later. He agreed that the story was not as bad as it could have been, and although he was concerned that the district attorney would be frustrated by the story being in the news, it was a somewhat sympathetic piece. He said that if they had contacted him for a statement, he would only have asked the reporter if the family hadn't suffered enough, which was exactly what the news anchor ended up saying.

I went to bed somewhat calmed, but found it hard to sleep. It was hard to find my balance in a life that didn't seem to stay still.

Such ups and downs plagued me, and made it harder for me to find rest. I laid in bed and asked God for peace and for wisdom about how to handle all of this. I asked God to take care of my son and help him rest. I wanted so much for my son on the eve of his 22nd birthday, and felt so powerless to help.

The next day, Clancy's birthday, was a Thursday, and it was Clancy's first full day of training in the firefighting program. I'd been so worried about the actual day being hard for him, and for all of us, but I realized that it was probably the perfect way to celebrate it. We'd do a family birthday dinner sometime during the weekend, but it was probably best that Clancy spend the actual day getting on with his own life. During the course of his 22 years there had been plenty of times when I controlled nearly every aspect of his existence. I'd been in charge of his food and clothing, sleeping and entertainment. His dad and I made up most of his world. But from here on out, I was definitely the passenger on this ride. There were limits to how much I could do for him. I had to trust Clancy. And God.

Two things encouraged me:

First, Clancy seemed to take to the firefighting program right away. Several of the other participants in his program struggled with the physical requirements of the course, but Clancy, in shape from years of hunting, camping, and construction work, breezed through the physical challenges. He did just as well in the technical aspects, acing his first written test without really studying. I felt that Clancy had come upon an important fork in the road that January, and his life went a different direction for a lot of reasons, many of which were out of his control. Nevertheless, the path he ended up choosing that month was a good one for him, and I was so glad to see him excelling in a field for which he seemed to have a natural aptitude.

Second—and this was a blessing I hadn't thought to expect—Clancy had a new girlfriend. After months of spending most of his time alone, he had met a young woman named Rachael. Rachel's stepmother was the aunt of Julie, Russ and Tracy's daughter-in-law, and Jeff, one of our closest friends. Rachael and Clancy had met at church, and I liked her right away. She was a student at the University of Colorado at Boulder, a gifted runner on CU's track team, and was studying integrative physiology. Her mother had died many years earlier, and Rachael was able to connect with Clancy in ways that a lot of other people couldn't. She helped him laugh and look forward to tomorrow. It was a new relationship, and I wasn't making any guesses about whether or not it would last in the long term, but I was grateful for her place in Clancy's life at the moment.

Living each new moment, one after the other. This was quickly becoming my approach to life.

CHAPTER 16

WINTER'S END

Winter's end is traditionally the season of renewal and rebirth. After the winter my family and I had lived through, both literally in snowy Colorado and metaphorically in our hearts, we all looked forward to a lifting of the darkness and the cold. As I'd learned in the previous months, however, the light comes back in small ways. The days get incrementally longer. Outside temperatures warm up a degree at a time. And this is the way through grief. You don't wake up one morning and suddenly feel hope or joy or peace. You just feel slightly less terrible, slightly less overwhelmed.

Ironically, when wading through grief, you'd think that the best course of action would be to just go away for a while and give yourself time to heal. I'm sure that would be a good plan for some people, and maybe would have made things easier for me, but it was never an option. Without a partner, there was more to do, not less.

On top of which, I had "widow's brain." Nothing seemed to stick in my head. I had trouble remembering what time school started, or what month it was. Occasionally I struggled coming up with the year. Forget about knowing what day of the week it might be. I just followed everyone else's lead on whether it was a church day, a workday or a home day.

I was talking with my sister one day about this and she told me that researchers had studied something called "transactive memory," in which the two partners in a couple eventually develop a shared store of knowledge that is stronger and more complex than the individual memories of either of them. In a shared memory, each partner doesn't have to know or remember everything. With Pat, I didn't have to know how to do maintenance on any of our vehicles. I didn't have to remember the passwords on the computer, or the day the phone bill was due. I didn't have to know how the well worked and how the sprinkler system tied into it. He had that covered. In reverse, I'm sure he didn't have a clue when James' next project was due or what it was about. I knew what time any major family event was held and where to go. I was sure to arrange dinner parties for the people at church he wanted to get to know. I made and purchased all the snacks for his monthly men's gathering at our house. We divided the work load. We carried our own amount of knowledge, but had access to the knowledge the other person carried.

I hadn't really appreciated how helpful this type of shared memory was until it was suddenly gone, which makes it both ironic and cruel that when you are in the middle of grieving the loss of someone, you simultaneously lose many of your available personal resources. That spring, between the closing of Pat's estate, the closing of Pat's business, the closing of both the Wolff House and the purchase of the townhouse, I was awash with paperwork. I carried around a pink plastic box with all the paperwork I needed to trudge through. I spent lunch hours going to the bank and the post office, signing and handing off documents. Tracy and I photocopied and faxed pages and pages of forms. We had to change the titles on all the cars, which meant arriving at the DMV before work to be first in line when they opened at 8 a.m. My mom worked with the probate attorney to make sure we complied with all the requirements of closing the estate, which were significant and time-consuming.

I knew that I was scrambling to meet the challenges of every day, and I often wondered how my kids were coping, especially since their mother seemed to be operating at about quarter-capacity.

James was so silent, it was especially hard to tell how he was doing. He quietly turned 14 years old in February and we had a low-key celebration, joining friends for dinner at a Chinese restaurant followed by a trip to Dairy Queen. He was never demanding, seeming to sense that I didn't have a lot of extra energy. Still, I wondered how he was coping inside all the silence.

Jesse was more outspoken. He shared a room with James in the apartment, which was hard for him. While James is a more typical teenager, happily living amidst piles of clothes and smelly baseball gear, Jesse is fastidious. He likes having his room clean and neat and works hard to keep it that way. This was a frequent source of tension between him and his brother. He was also trying to get Pat's truck working. He became even more passionate about his love of trucks and cars, Fords specifically. He spent all his free time researching vehicles.

Sadie was back on track with her college program, taking classes on different culinary arts. I worried about her driving in the ice and snow to class every morning at 5:30 a.m., but she still seemed to enjoy her program and we started talking about opening a cafe together someday. We had begun tossing around the idea after Sadie started at the culinary school, but since our house project was now gone, we began daydreaming about a different future. We would visit coffee shops and take notes on things we liked.

Clancy worried me. He still wasn't sleeping regularly and had lost a lot of weight. He was busy with his firefighting program, which was good, but it meant that I didn't hear from him regularly. One afternoon, when I hadn't heard from him for a few days, I tried calling him. He didn't answer his phone. I kept calling off and on into the evening. Still no answer. I went out for the evening and tried calling him again after I got home. Still no answer! I must have left him 20 voice mails and as many text messages. He didn't have a roommate and I didn't know of anyone living in his vicinity that I could call to go check on him. I had already gotten into my pajamas and removed my contacts, but I knew I couldn't sleep without knowing he was okay. Horrible images crowded my tired brain. By 11 p.m., it was snowing again, but I debated driving over icy roads to his apartment to check on him. Just as I was about to leave my house, he finally answered. He'd fallen asleep on his couch that afternoon and had slept through all of my calls.

The date for Clancy's second hearing with the deputy district attorney was scheduled for February. As the day loomed, I thought more and more about our initial meeting with John Kendrick and how uncomfortable he seemed around Clancy and me. There was no way I could have known exactly what he felt, but I had the feeling that he had been given directions to "throw the book" at Clancy and was struggling with himself not to be sympathetic toward his situation. It was almost as if his hands were tied, and he had to work himself up to be stern in our presence.

I wasn't sure why Kendrick would be instructed to act this way, but the more I heard about his boss, District Attorney Smith, the more it made sense. Apparently, she felt that she had been elected to take a "tough on crime" stance, and to use almost any method to do so. She had been accused of compensating witnesses in trials. Ethics charges had been filed against her. She had built a reputation for being ruthless and uncompromising, and for disregarding the specific circumstances of individual cases. None of these factors helped my son.

I shared my impressions with Gary, Clancy's attorney, and asked him if he felt it would be more productive if Clancy and I weren't in the room when he met with Kendrick. Gary agreed. On the day of the second hearing, although Clancy and I both made the long drive to Hugo, Gary went into Kendrick's office alone and we sat outside. Gary would call us in if he felt it was necessary.

Apparently this was a good strategy because the deputy district attorney seemed much more relaxed and open meeting Gary alone. He appeared to be more sympathetic to Clancy's situation and willing to consider a plea bargain, something he had previously said was off the table. For the first time, he said he would consider a "deferred judgment," in which sentencing would be deferred until after Clancy completed a probationary period. These terms would probably involve a loss of his driver's license, community service and a year's probation. If Clancy completed all the terms, the charge would be erased completely. This was obviously a much more appealing option than a trial to us, but Kendrick told Gary that he would have to "sell" the idea to the district attorney, and he was unsure she would go for it.

At the February hearing, Gary also finally learned at least one of the reasons Smith seemed to be taking an especially aggressive approach to Clancy's case, one in which there was no evidence of guilt or criminal behavior. Smith was apparently frustrated with what she perceived as the "good old boy" network among the lawyers and politicians in Colorado. It was a system she seemed determined to disregard. Therefore, when her office received calls from Jack Woodward, a congressman for Colorado, she interpreted the contact as an effort to unduly influence her and her office, rather than as a call from a family friend who felt a young man had been unfairly targeted. Perhaps Jack's phone call had the unfortunate effect of leading Smith to react even more harshly in Clancy's case.

The next hearing was set for April, over two months away. We really weren't too upset about the delay. It had appeared that the longer we waited, the more options became available to us. We were hopeful that we were on the right track. Clancy still had his driver's license and could still go to school.

Clancy and I drove home from Hugo feeling lighter than we

had on the way over. For the first time Clancy thought that he might not have to go to trial. It was a small blessing, but I would take any I could get.

Getting to Know
James

J ames is my youngest son, and the most unexpected of all my children. Having had three children already, all of them difficult births, my doctor had advised me to stop, suggesting that we consider our family complete. Yet I never really felt that we were finished. There was still another space to fill.

This was the situation in the winter of 1997. Pat and I had just sat down at our picnic-style dinner table to eat dinner with our three young children, when I realized with complete annoyance that my feet were freezing. I jumped up and headed down the hall toward my bedroom to get some slippers. As I stepped through the door to my bedroom, I noticed that the light on the answering machine was blinking. I had a message. I loved the mystery of wondering who had called. It was like Christmas! I could not have known that this time that feeling would be truer than ever again in my life. I pressed "Play" as I entered my walk-in closet to fetch my slippers and heard an unfamiliar voice speaking.

"Hi. My name is Steve Griswold, from the Denver Department of Social Services."

Oh, no!! My mind raced. Someone had surely reported me

for child abuse for spanking one of my kids in the bathroom at WalMart. The voice continued, "I am looking for a placement home for your sister Karen's son, James."

"What?" I thought. I hadn't heard from Karen in years. *Who was James? How old is he? Where is Karen? Dead? In the hospital?* So many questions.

The voice continued, "Please call me at -------." I listened to the message again to make sure I didn't miss any important information.

When I returned to the table I must have looked bewildered. Pat asked who had called and I explained the message to Pat while the kids continued eating. I don't know if they could possibly understand the implications of this phone call. Pat starting asking all the same questions that had just run through in my head.

When Karen and I were in high school, Karen didn't have many friends, and my parents were afraid that the ones she did have would drag her into trouble. My parents would only let her attend functions for school and church if she went with Pat and me. Looking back now, I'm not sure why Pat agreed to have my sister tag along on many of our dates, but he did. As a result, both Pat and I had spent a lot of time with Karen. Even though we knew nothing about this unknown child James, we had both spent a lot of time with the woman who had given birth to him.

The timing of the call was amazing. Just the night before, Pat and I had decided to try to adopt another child. I had always been interested in adopting a baby girl from China, but I wasn't sure if Pat felt the same way. Incredibly, the day before, Pat had gone into a gas station to buy coffee, as he did most days. A small Chinese girl about three years old looked up at him and smiled. That's all it took for him to be convinced. We had just spent the entire previous evening discussing how we could make this happen. We'd heard this process was costly. We could sell our house and use the equity to adopt.

And then we got the call about James.

I tried to return Steve Griswold's call that night, but it was after business hours and no one answered. Pat and I slept fitfully because our minds raced with all the possibilities. The next morning, I took Clancy and Sadie to school at 7:40 and was sure to be home to return the call at eight o'clock when the Department of Social Services opened. Steve was in and took my call.

I learned that my sister Karen had had a baby two days earlier, and because of unresolved issues in her life, they were unwilling to let James go home with her. Denver County was starting a new program called kinship care. Steve explained that while birth mothers were getting their lives together, they placed babies with family members. I was the only sibling that Karen said she had.

Why had she said that? We had two other siblings. In addition, Karen had given them our parent's old telephone number, which Pat and I took over when my parents went out of town. Karen couldn't have known that.

Steve told me that if we agreed to try this program, we could pick up this little baby named James the following Thursday. I told Steve that I'd need to discuss these things with my husband and would call him back.

After hanging up the phone, I called Pat and filled him in. The phrase "it takes a village to raise a child" hadn't yet become popular. I don't know for sure if it takes a village but I knew it would take a family! I phoned my mom and dad. I called Tracy. I called both of my other sisters. Throughout that day we all devised a plan that would allow us to take James home. I was working two and a half days a week at that time, but my mom already watched my other kids on two of my work days, while Tracy helped with the half-day. They both agreed to add James to my clan. Also, to keep my family from feeling overwhelmed, my sister Karla agreed to keep James overnight once a week, as did my parents.

A nagging thought kept disrupting our planning. Could I love another baby as much as I loved my biological children? I'm not sure why it seemed so important to me. This arrangement was only supposed to be temporary. Still, I couldn't let the nagging thought go. I called Steve Griswold and asked him if I could go to the hospital to see this baby before I committed to bringing him home. It seemed simple. If I looked at him, I would know if I could love him, right? Steve told me that a visit wasn't possible.

That night Pat and I talked at length about the journey ahead of us and the possible reasons God might have done this. Was it to actively have our influence back in Karen's life? Maybe it was so we could impact this new program at Denver social services. Our thoughts at that time were only about how we could have an impact on others. We couldn't know, but we felt as if God had, for whatever reason, put this opportunity before us. We couldn't say no.

We woke up the next morning, rushing around as usual. After dropping Clancy and Sadie off at school, I met Tracy and my mom at the nearest Starbucks for coffee. I left Jesse with my mom and went the short distance to work. All my friends at work were so excited and offered to help by bringing meals and coming over to help with the new baby.

During the day I realized how much I needed to do to get ready. Most people get months of notice before bringing a baby home and I only had days. Just the weekend before the phone call, I had taken down Jesse's crib. He was two and a half and ready for a big boy bed. And, because we had tentatively planned to adopt a little girl from China, I didn't need baby boy clothes, so I'd given all of ours away.

While I was at work that day my mom did something that totally represents the role she had always played in my family. She went to Walmart with Jesse in tow and bought diapers, baby clothes, pacifiers, a baby swing, and a car seat. When I got home it was like I'd had a baby shower. I washed all the clothes and bottles and prepared to have a new little one in the house.

Although I was getting more used to the idea, the question still pestered me: Could I love a baby I hadn't given birth to in the same way that I loved Clancy, Sadie, and Jesse?

The next morning came quickly, and I was ready. I'd asked Tracy to join me because I was sure I was unfit to be alone with my thoughts. She and I spent the day together running errands, then picked up Clancy, Sadie and Elizabeth, with Jesse strapped securely in his car seat. Finally, Tracy drove us to the foster home without any trouble and we sat in the driveway in our mini van.

We left the kids in the car with Clancy in charge, and Tracy and I went to the door and rang the bell. A petite older woman answered. She seemed much too old to be caring for small children, let alone getting up in the night with a new baby. The bi-level house smelled of dirty diapers and cigarettes. We could hear the noises of small children coming from areas that we couldn't even see. Baby gates separated all the rooms. The women very casually picked up James and put him in my arms. He came with nothing. We thanked the woman and left quickly. We couldn't wait to get home to get a closer look at this new addition to our family.

The first thing we did once we got James into the house was fill the kitchen sink with warm water and throw in the new bottle of lavender-scented baby wash to warm it. The kids all gathered

around in the kitchen hoping to get a closer look. James was little, just about seven pounds. We finished bathing him, and set him on a towel next to the sink to slather him with the matching lavender-scented lotion. His blonde hair was fine, but he had a lot of it and it stuck straight up. He had my sister's eyes—beautiful, deep-set, and blue. His tiny little fingers were exact replicas of Karen's as well. We dressed him in his new little onesie and a sleeper and wrapped him up like a burrito in a receiving blanket. I cradled him tightly in my arms and just intentionally embraced the moment.

That was it! I was in love! I had to protect him and care for him just the same way that I had been doing for the past nine years with my other three children.

Just as quickly, my fear about being able to love this tiny baby was replaced by another one:

Would I lose him?

This fear stayed with me through his whole first year. Little did I know that it was also the fear of his new siblings, cousins, aunts, uncles, and grandparents as well. One day, while driving in the minivan, I looked in the rearview mirror to see Sadie tearing up. I asked her what was wrong.

"What if we have to give him back? What will happen to him?"

She was really frightened at the thought. I could tell that it was a selfless thought—not at her loss of a brother, but real concern for his future.

The fears ended when James was about a year old. While Karen began on a better path after his birth, it didn't last. About six months later she disappeared again. The County motioned to relinquish all rights to James, and by the time he was a year old, it was granted. The adoption process began. During this entire time we had a revolving door of social workers in and out of our home. Life with four kids often looks like complete chaos and I was nervous. However, the social worker on our case for the first year got so comfortable with us that she wouldn't even knock, and just come bursting through the door. Every time, without exception, the house was peaceful. No crying. No fighting. Complete order! How can this be? I thought it was a miracle.

The social worker gave us some advice that resonated with me. She said that we should all wish the best for the sister that birthed James and hope that she gets it all figured out. We just believe that she didn't do it in time to be his parent. For James to have the best shot at a normal childhood, she advised us that we should not have contact with Karen. This was something of a moot point. We didn't know where she was or how to contact her anyway.

"He has siblings and nineteen cousins," she said. "He has twelve very involved aunts and uncles and two of the best sets of grandparents any one could want. His little life is full of love."

Around the time of James' second birthday, we packed the courtroom at the final adoption hearing. The judge was truly moved.

Being the youngest child, James got to spend the least time with his dad, but what he had was special and different than the other three kids. When James was a baby, he seemed to have only one special need: to be held. He was a perfectly content baby as long as he was in someone's arms. As a working mother of four and all that entails, I couldn't hold him in the evenings. I was bathing kids, doing dishes, helping with school projects. So Pat held him every night for hours. There was such a bond between them. Maybe God knew that this was what they both needed.

James had tremendous hand/eye coordination from the time he was little and threw balls from the time he was a year old. This ended up in an interest in baseball. Pat was excited to help James develop this talent and ended up helping coach his team for many years. This allowed the two of them to ride alone to practice every day and to games. I'm so grateful for the time James and Pat spent together.

We never intended to be secretive about how James came to be a part of our family, but we realized when he was four that he didn't know. It was Christmas time and I had just purchased the new Steven Curtis Chapman cd. I peeled off the cellophane packaging, opened the case and began reading the inside cover. It talked about how the Chapman's family life had been blessed through the adoption of precious little girls from China. What I was reading was exactly how Pat and I felt. Initially, when James first came into our lives, we arrogantly wondered about the ways in which we could positively impact other lives, especially the life of our son, James. Now, many years later we could totally see that it was the other way around. There were definitely other people

who could have been more qualified parents for him. There were people who could have given him more than we could. But we were the ones who had been blessed by this child, by this situation, by that first phone call. God granted us a gift that we would never have asked for on our own. When James was almost nine years old, we decided we couldn't wait any longer to tell him I didn't give birth to him.

We wrote him his own book, calling it *Sweet Baby James*, and asked for contributions from the wide circle of people who love him and are his family. We talked about how we had been blessed by his presence in our lives.

James was thirteen when I got that other life-altering phone call and learned that Pat had been killed in a car accident. In the

years since that day, James has grown into a charming, funny young man. It is a special gift of his. We all need some comic relief given the hard reality of life. The other kids are adults and mostly doing their own thing. But James is still with me. God knew I would need him to keep me company and keep me laughing for a few more years now that I'm suddenly single.

I no longer get excited when the phone rings. I usually get scared. Maybe I should remember that this great gift started with a phone call. I'm going to try to react differently. Thank you God for revealing this to me! Thank you God for my sweet baby James!

CHAPTER 17

A NEW HOME

The Wolff house was finally finished. I stepped onto the front porch with its gleaming paint and crossed to the front door. I slid the key in the lock and opened it, the ornate brass of the doorknob polished and bright, and stepped inside. The old wood floors glowed under fresh varnish and the sunlight poured through the windows, lighting up the pale yellow walls of the living room. I walked through the dining room, my footsteps echoing in the empty spaces, and entered the newly remodeled kitchen. I ran my hands over the granite countertops, opened and closed the doors on a few of the newly installed cabinets. It was all so beautiful.

I remembered standing in the very spot with Pat just six months earlier, looking around at cracked plaster and warped cabinets, but seeing instead the vision of what we thought it would be. This kitchen, as lovely as it was, was not what we had expected, nor what we had planned. But I had learned that plans can change in a moment, and your options are to either to change your plans or to break. The Wolff house had obviously been intended to be someone else's home, and I had no doubt that it would be a beautiful place for a family. Just not mine.

I left the keys on the counter for the new owners and walked out the door, letting it lock behind me.

We had arranged that the closing on the Wolff house would happen on March 16th, the day before I closed on our new townhouse. I didn't realize until later that the townhouse closing was on March 17th, St. Patrick's Day, which seemed appropriate.

I woke up on the day of the townhouse closing and laid in bed thinking. I had such mixed feelings. I remembered the day Pat and I closed on the Wolff house. We were both so excited we could barely sleep. I couldn't wait to finish signing the paperwork and get the keys so we could start working on our new home. This time felt different. Yes, I was looking forward to having a new home for my children and myself, and grateful that the circumstances had worked out so well, but it was still hard to feel much excitement about anything, even a new home.

Complicating matters was the fact that I had decided that I would not bring our two dogs, Lily and Dudley, into the new house with us. Both dogs were quite old and had significant health problems. The vet had recommended putting them down, and I waited until the transition into the new house to do so. So, on the morning of the closing, Sadie and I drove both dogs to the Dumb Friends League, held them in our arms for final hugs, and then had them put to sleep. We took their little collars with us, got in the car, and cried all the way home. Intellectually, I felt that I had made the right decision. Emotionally, however, it was still hard. Yet every day was hard. This loss, in the midst of everything we had already said goodbye to, seemed to merge with the rest.

My parents came and picked me up at the apartment and drove me to the bank. My dad waited in the car while my mom came with me to sign the papers. We drove straight home afterward and started moving out of the apartment and into the townhouse. Clancy came over and helped move the heaviest pieces—Pat's antique bookcase and desk he always used—and my parents, Sadie and the boys and I moved everything else. We were literally moving just a few hundred feet away and for the next few days carried boxes down the street to the new house. Mom and Dad helped us shampoo carpets and clean up the old apartment. I handed off the apartment keys at the rental office.

Our lives in the new place didn't feel all that different. The boys each had more space, which was an instant improvement, but not much else had changed. I still carpooled with Tracy to work several days a week. Sadie and the boys still drove the same route to school. But other things had changed. This time, the place was ours. We talked about painting walls and decorating. We talked about how we would use the patio in the summer. Still, it was the first home I had ever owned without Pat, and it would take me a little while to get used to the idea.

Clancy's next hearing was scheduled for April 7th. Just as we had done twice before, I took the day off of work and Clancy and I made the two-hour drive to Hugo to meet with Gary and John

Kendrick. Just as before, we agreed that Gary would meet with the deputy district attorney by himself. After waiting for several hours, Gary was finally called in to the meeting. They got right to the negotiations. Kendrick might agree to a deferred judgment if Clancy would agree to the terms of probation for a period of three years. Clancy would face a suspension of his driver's license for at least one year. He would be required to perform community service, which would involve weekly meetings with a parole officer in Hugo, and he would be restricted from carrying or using any sort of firearm and using any alcohol for the duration of the probationary period. These were the four variables, and the negotiations began over how much Clancy would be asked to give in each area.

We drove home once again, feeling more comfortable that Clancy could avoid a risky and costly trial, but unhappy with the remaining options available to us. There were serious consequences for all of the conditions of the probationary period.

From my own perspective, I was most concerned about the suspension of his license. Kendrick initially wanted to take Clancy's license at least one year. I wanted something significantly shorter. That punishment was not only hard on Clancy, but hard on me. I depended on Clancy to help me shuttle my kids around and would miss his help in that area. In addition, with Clancy unable to drive, the burden would fall back on me to help get him places. Plus, I was concerned that it would be even harder for Clancy to go back to school and/or get a job without being able to provide his own transportation.

The second condition, community service, was less of a problem. Clancy had been doing community service on his own for years, and in fact wanted a career in community service. We were concerned, however, about where the community service would be required. Without being able to drive, Clancy would prefer a site near his house. At this point, we weren't at all certain that the probation officer would be reasonable on this score. Kendrick had started out with the idea of performing 25 hours of service, but Clancy considered this his leverage; he would be willing to do significantly more service—up to 200 hours—in exchange for reduced license suspension or some flexibility on the gun restrictions.

In fact, the gun restrictions were the most troublesome for Clancy. A standard term prohibits anyone on probation from drinking alcohol or carrying or using a firearm during the probation period. It didn't matter that neither guns nor alcohol were at issue in the accident, the requirement would be imposed on him anyway. Clancy didn't have a problem with the alcohol requirement, but the restriction against firearms was almost more upsetting than the loss of his license. Clancy regularly worked security at our church and for many of the private events that used the church building as a venue. Clancy had years of gun training and a concealed carry permit. He would not be able to work security during the probation.

Most important of all was that he would temporarily have to give up hunting, which had been an important activity to him since his dad had died. He felt connected to his father when he was out hunting, and was able to leave his troubles behind him even for a short while. Giving up hunting, even temporarily, was an enormous loss, and one that almost no one else truly understood. Clancy would be willing to do more community service or to add to his driving restrictions if he could only be able to go hunting again.

These were the variables we had to work with, and Gary and Kendrick would spend the next several weeks going back and forth in negotiations. Up to 200 hours community service but only 4 months' loss of license. Kendrick liked the community service and was impressed Clancy would be willing to do it, but would still require 8 months without a license. Gary asked if they would modify the probation to allow Clancy to go hunting. Kendrick said he'd see what he could do.

And there was still the option of rejecting the plea bargain altogether and going to trial. It was a terrible option, involving thousands and thousands of dollars I didn't have, jeopardizing Josh's career as he would surely be called to testify, and risking a guilty sentence for Clancy. But it was tempting. In the midst of these negotiations, we heard a rumor that the district attorney had instituted a bonus system for her deputies for taking cases to trial and winning convictions. Gary had also heard this rumor. Many people were outraged by this and wanted to expose the story to the media, but by this point I was really afraid of what sort of retaliation Clancy might face if we accused her publicly.

Gary was outraged. Nothing about the case made sense based on his experience as a criminal lawyer and what he knew about the case. Gary had a friend who had been a career prosecutor who was so furious about the way the district attorney's office was pursuing Clancy's case that he told Gary he would volunteer his time to help should we choose to go to trial.

Gary himself had mixed feelings about accepting a plea

bargain. He felt that Clancy had a strong case and, conversely, that the district attorney had a weak one. He told me that he regularly rehearsed the arguments he would make to a jury, and believed that he could win at a trial. Still, he had a responsibility to his client. Clancy's primary objective was to preserve his career opportunities. Gary reminded us that Clancy could lose if we were to go to trial, and maybe a plea bargain would be a better option. As Gary said, "sometimes a bad plea bargain is better than a good trial."

I asked Gary what he would do if his son were being charged. Gary told me he would take the plea bargain, but he would try to improve it.

I knew in my heart that Gary was right. A plea bargain that protected Clancy's options in the long run was probably the best call. I just wasn't sure I could bear seeing Clancy stand up in front of a judge and say that he was guilty. I decided I would have to deal with that when the time came.

Less than a week later, an incident happened that confirmed for me, and I think for Clancy, that despite all the roadblocks being placed in his way, the path he was on seemed right for him. He had driven to the nearby town of Boulder for the evening to visit his girlfriend Rachael at the University of Colorado. He was driving back home on a mountain highway, thinking about how dark and rutted the road was and how surprising it was that there weren't more accidents on it.

Suddenly, the car directly in front of him swerved. Clancy looked to see what the driver was trying to avoid and saw a dark sedan on its roof at the side of the road. Half of the car was on the shoulder of the road, while half of it was in the roadway. It was nearly impossible to see.

A couple of cars had already stopped, and Clancy pulled over as well. Because he was in training at the fire-fighting academy, he had all of his bunker gear—jacket, pants, boots and helmet—in his truck. He quickly decided that if the driver was still trapped in the car and it caught on fire, he'd be in a better position than most to offer assistance. Plus, he just wanted to help.

For some reason, he felt a sense of urgency to get to the scene and ran to the overturned car. There were four people standing next to the car, including, he was told, the driver. Everyone had made it out of the car and appeared to be okay, but he noticed that some sort of fluid was leaking from the car and that one of the bystanders was smoking a cigarette. This, combined with the group's exposure on the side of a dark road, seemed very unsafe. He moved the group about 100 yards away from the site of the accident.

Less than fifteen seconds after the group moved, a van traveling down the road hit the portion of the overturned car that was still in the road. The impact smashed the passenger side of the van and sent the overturned car spinning on its top. If Clancy hadn't moved the bystanders, the spinning car would have hit them.

The van that hit the sedan continued a little ways up the road and then stopped. Clancy rushed to the van. Although the driver seemed uninjured, the passenger side of the van was smashed, the windshield was shattered and the door was jammed shut. Clancy saw an an older gentleman inside, bleeding from his forehead and his nose. He was conscious, but not responding or coherent.

Worried that the man might have a concussion, Clancy pried the door open, helped him from the car, and sat down on the ground next to him. He sat with the man until the first responders arrived.

Once the state troopers and firefighters arrived, Clancy shared what he had observed and what steps he had taken. He waited until the driver of the sedan and the passenger in the van were taken away by ambulance. After checking in with the officers and firefighters on site to make sure there was nothing else he could do, he drove home.

Clancy called me that evening to tell me what had happened. I could tell he was pleased to have been able to step into the situation with confidence and some skills. After months of waiting to see what would happen to him, he seemed eager to have been able to do something positive for someone else.

I was grateful as well to see that the next time Clancy had faced a car accident, just six months after his own, he hadn't frozen or felt afraid. He'd run right into the thick of it without even hesitating. This work was good for him.

CHAPTER 18

THE JOY OF COOKING

Mother's Day, 2011. I didn't really feel like I wanted to celebrate the holiday. I was barely keeping up with running my own life and had very little energy left over to commit to parenthood. I felt guilty and alone, and Mother's Day felt like a recrimination, not the flowers and breakfast-in-bed occasion suggested by Hallmark. I woke up and wrote down a quick prayer:

> *Today is the hardest holiday to bear so far. Jesus, get me through this one too, please, without displeasing you. Give me the faith to truly believe that your ways are for me and my children's ultimate good. Give me the wisdom to parent these babies without their strong dad, especially the boys since even after having three of them, I still don't get how they are wired. Help me to comfort them and encourage them! Thank you Jesus for these four beautiful babies.*

I struggled with the fact that I wasn't able to be the kind of parent I wanted to be. I knew that my children needed my support now more than ever, just at a time when I was least able to give it. Every once in a while I tried to stop, take a moment to focus on what they were all doing, and acknowledge how hard they were all working. I remember one morning feeling particularly overwhelmed and just spent a few minutes sending them messages on Facebook:

To: James McKendry

Go get em today! Look alive! Roll a pair. See it and drive it! Sorry I can't be there you goofy goober! Love ya!

To: Sadie McKendry

When you get home tonight.... show me what you learned in school today! Loving what you're learning, my sweet darling girl!

To: Jesse McKendry

Thank you for making sure James gets where he needs to! I couldn't make it without you, Bud!! Romans 13:1: "A wise son hears his father's instruction." Your dad gave you enough instruction. Just keep it in the front of your mind always! The rest of that chapter's good too. Read it today please! I'm grateful for you and you make my heart glad. Have a good day!

To: Clancy McKendry

My precious baby boy, the one passage highlighted in your daddy's bible, is "Marks of a True Christian," Romans 12:9-21: "Bless those who persecute you, repay no one evil for evil, as far as it depends on you, live peaceably with all. Never avenge yourself, but leave it to the wrath of God. Vengeance is mine sayeth the Lord. Do not overcome evil with evil but overcome evil with good! You're the light on a hill, the salt of the earth, my darling and u r *definitely in the spotlight!!!! Love ya to the moon!!*

More than anything, I wanted my children to have hope for what was coming and a sense of purpose. I wanted them to feel God's direction in their lives and have something to look forward to and prepare for.

I wanted that for myself, too. But whereas my children were expected to look forward to new relationships and jobs, I thought I had already figured all of those things out for myself. It was so, so strange to feel like I was starting everything over at 44 years old. What relationships would be in my future? What jobs? What would my new mission be?

One idea kept floating around in my mind. During the previous winter when everyone pitched in to help remodel the Wolff house, I knew that I wanted to come up with some way to thank people for their selfless support. A simple thank you note seemed inadequate in response to the amount of time and money that was poured out on my family's behalf. I wanted to do more, but had so little energy—or time.

And yet, in the middle of that difficult winter, an idea bubbled up: a Thank You Dinner! If there was anything that gave me a little bounce of joy back then, it was the idea of planning meals or parties with Sadie. What if Sadie and I catered this dinner? We could hold it in the reception hall at the church, the same space where we had gathered after Pat's memorial service. The boys could help with food prep, set up, and serving. The church kitchen was tiny, but we could make it work. Maybe we could rent all the dishes and cutlery, borrow serving pieces from friends. I could hire some of the kids' friends to help serve.

I felt a tiny glimmer of excitement. There was something calming, creative, and joyful about cooking that Sadie and I had always shared. In fact, this had been a big part of the ministry Pat and I had—gathering groups of people around food.

I realized that cooking had also been somewhat therapeutic for us as well. Even during those first few weeks after Pat died, our friend Corrie Casey, who was also a caterer, had invited Sadie over on almost a weekly basis to cook together. Then we would all get together and eat what they had prepared. There is something about cooking and presenting food that feeds my soul as well as my body. It gathers people together. It creates community.

I finally figured out that we could thank people by doing the thing that gave me the most joy.

This was part of a question I had played with for years. I had often wondered about the things that God called us to do. Would we be willing to do anything God asked of us, no matter how difficult or unappealing the task? Would I be willing to go anywhere God sent me, do any kind of work that was given to me? Certainly, we are asked to bear unbelievable burdens in life, such as to keep moving forward after your young husband is killed in a car accident. We are asked to stay faithful even when our children are falsely charged with a crime. Life is hard, and we are asked to stay strong in the face of it.

But what about our ministry? Our life's work? Are we called to do the impossible or the distasteful? This I couldn't believe. I believe that God uses me as me. God gives us the desires of our hearts—not just the objects of the desires, but the actual desires. And God had given me a joy in serving people food.

I remember a conversation I had with a few of the missionary women we visited in Loiyangalani, Kenya. We were sitting in the kitchen of one of their homes, and I wondered aloud if I would be willing to work in Africa if I felt that God had called us there. It would seem like a hard choice to make, and one that felt more scary and hard than inviting. Jim and Barb Teasdale had often spoken to us about all of their adventures in that life, and the snakes alone were enough for me to be sure I was not called to Africa. I told these women how much I admired them for their sacrifices, for giving up the good life to serve the many tribes of people there.

Big mistake!

What I had just done was offend them, especially one woman in particular. Although many of the missionaries had spent time in our church, and even stayed in our home, this was one woman I didn't already know.

"This is right where we desire to be!" she said in an annoyed tone. "In fact if we were in the States, we would be unhappy."

I then began to understand God's calling to ministry a bit differently. These women were doing what they were suited for, what they were passionate about.

Had anyone ever been called to be a caterer? A cook? I felt certain that this was true for Sadie. Never had I seen someone so inspired to create with food. She is truly talented and motivated and has the training to support it. But me? I didn't know. All I knew was that I felt drawn to, excited even, by the idea of preparing a meal in gratitude for the people who had helped me.

We scheduled the dinner for a Friday night in May. We invited over 80 people, thinking that with all the commitments everyone had, only about 50 or so would be able to make it. My niece Katherine offered to make the invitations for the event. We copied the color scheme and the design from Pat's favorite pink paisley shirt. He always got grief from the men in our church when he had it on, but he didn't let that deter him from wearing it. A lot! The invitations also carried verses from the scripture passage Pat had underlined in his Bible. We sealed and stamped the invitations and sent them out, waiting to find out our final numbers so we could plan for the night of the dinner.

Almost every single person we invited said they could come, a total of 82. We were surprised, pleased, and a little overwhelmed, thinking about how we could cook for, serve, and feed that many people. Corrie agreed to help cook the different courses in the tiny kitchen at the church. My sisters, their husbands and some of their kids flew out to help with the dinner, and together we set up tables that filled the reception hall. Floral centerpieces sat atop linen covered tables. At each place setting was a small, dark blue box inside which nestled two chocolate covered sea salt caramels from a recipe Sadie had perfected over the winter. It was our parting gift to each of the people attending.

People started arriving, and they were seated and served by my boys, several of their cousins, and some of their friends, all dressed in chef coats and black pants. We frantically plated up servings of ribboned carrots served on butter lettuce, mango chutney pepper steak, heavenly potatoes in paisley forms, and white and green asparagus.

At the end of the dinner came a dessert trio of a chocolate truffle, a Nutella pavlova with a raspberry and mint leaf on top, and a lemon cookie, all accompanied by coffee and my mom's homemade peach-apricot wine. Sadie and I stood up in front of the crowd of friends, family, electricians, painters, plumbers and assorted helpers to say two things. First, we thanked all of our guests for rising to meet the needs of my family in such an immediate, selfless, and consistent way. It really was an honor to have the group gathered before me, and to see the faces of all the people who had come together for no other reason than to honor Pat and to help my family.

Second, Sadie and I announced the launch of our new, fledgling catering company. We decided that this was something we could do part-time while she finished school and I continued to work at the dental office. During the spring, while we were working out the details of our Thank You Dinner, we were also figuring out the details of our new business. We would cater small dinners and parties on evenings and weekends. We also explored trying to sell Sadie's Sea Salt Caramels, just like the ones that sat at each place setting. We were starting small, that's for sure, uncertain about whether this was a long-term adventure or just one that felt good right now. Either way, it marked a step toward a different future for us, and for me.

We struggled a bit longer with what to call our business. We wanted it to be easy to say and easy to remember. We wanted it to reflect the work we were trying to do and the story of what it took to get us to this point in our lives. In the end, we came up with something we liked. Our friend Simon designed our business cards, a copy of which was attached to each box of caramels we were giving our guests. The design included an element of the pink paisley, swirled around the name of our executive catering company. It was simple and fitting:

Rise.

CHAPTER 19

THE HEARING

June 14, 2011. Clancy got up that morning and made a long, last trip to Hugo, Colorado, for his first and only hearing before a judge.

It had taken so much time and energy to get to this day. Since the last hearing in April, Clancy's attorney had been doing a lot of back and forth negotiations. Kendrick had finally agreed to a deferred judgment so that the charges would be erased after Clancy completed the terms set out for him. What took a long time was figuring out exactly what those terms would be.

At the very least, Kendrick was requiring a one-year probation. Clancy would have to be so careful, avoiding trouble of any kind. Also, state law required regular monthly check-in appointments with a parole officer, regular drug tests, and year-long restrictions against both alcohol and gun use. After weeks of negotiation, Kendrick still required a full eight-month restriction on

Clancy's driver's license, but he agreed to have Clancy voluntarily surrender it instead of having the restriction registered with the DMV.

Finally, Clancy would be required to complete 100 hours of community service. We had offered the large number of community service hours at the suggestion of our attorney. Clancy didn't mind doing community service, but he wasn't sure how he was going to complete it without transportation.

And finally, he would not be able to use his guns during the entire probation period. Although it was within the deputy district attorney's power to adjust the restriction, he chose not to. The most he was willing to consider was to allow Clancy to go bow hunting instead. It seemed like quite a blow.

Gary continued to push, asking to reduce the loss of Clancy's driver's license, and to ease the gun restrictions. He reminded Kendrick that Clancy agreed to the 100 hours of community service, raised from the original 25. He reasoned that limiting Clancy's driving ability punished me more than it punished Clancy. But Kendrick was unmoved.

"Don't make me regret offering the deferred judgment," was his final reply. This was the deal. Clancy could accept it or take the case to trial.

After eight months of having a criminal charge hanging over Clancy's head, we were all ready for it to be resolved. To this day, both Clancy and I believe that he would have been acquitted had the case gone to trial. A verdict of "not guilty" would have felt so much better, releasing Clancy not only of the obligations to complete a sentence of any sort, but also relieving him of the cloud of blame that I felt hovered over him. It all seemed so unnecessary, so cruel. I couldn't understand how he could be made to feel even worse about the tragic loss of his father.

And yet, after talking with Clancy's attorney and many trusted family members and friends, we decided to take the plea agreement. The trial would be both costly and still carried the risk that Clancy would lose. The plea bargain would at least place the control over Clancy's future back into his own hands. He would know exactly what he needed to do to clear his name. We decided that it was time he moved forward. The sooner he started the probationary period, the sooner he could be finished with it.

The attorneys scheduled the hearing with the judge for June 14, 2011 at 10:00 in the morning. All we needed now was for the judge to agree with what the attorneys had negotiated.

Clancy's attorney recommended that I not be in the courtroom. Instinctively, I knew he was right. I could not bear to hear my son say the word "guilty" about the accident. We arranged to have our good friend, Collin Myrick, attend the hearing with Clancy and his attorney.

The night before the hearing, I posted a request for prayers on Facebook:

> *Very big, difficult day tomorrow in Hugo, so please pray for the right words, peace in the middle of the storm, God's attending to be very obvious. I'm still praying for a miracle, but recognizing that God might choose to use my baby to glorify Himself, in what appears less miraculous from my perspective.*

In my heart I was hoping that the judge would see Clancy's situation as unjust and throw the whole thing out, but I knew enough not to expect it. The next morning, I dressed in scrubs and went to work at the dental office while Clancy dressed in nice slacks and a dress shirt and drove to Hugo. When the judge called his name, Clancy stood with Gary and said the words I could not bear to hear.

All morning, I kept my phone with me while I was working with patients. It was close to lunch time when I felt the vibration of my phone ringing. I quickly called someone to cover for me and took my phone call into the staff lounge. It was Gary. He told me that everything had gone as we'd expected, if not as we had hoped. The judge accepted all the terms as the attorneys had negotiated, even granting Clancy the right to go bow hunting. Then Gary put Clancy on the phone and we chatted briefly. He seemed okay.

I was experiencing such a wide range of emotions at that very moment. I was relieved to hear a calmness in Clancy's voice. I was very disappointed that the case didn't get thrown out. I was scared that Clancy wouldn't make it through the year.

When I talked to Clancy later, he told me that standing up and pleading guilty that morning was the hardest thing he had ever had to do. But he did it to be done with the ambiguity, and to be able to move on. It was over. At least we had a decision.

He later said that there was also another outcome of that day in the courtroom: his attachment to the criminal justice system was gone forever. As much as he had at one time been committed to a career as a police officer, he couldn't see himself working in it. As he left the courtroom on June 14, 2011, he turned away from the road that led toward criminal justice. He would still serve, just not in the way he originally thought.

I was happy for Clancy that the clock was now ticking. In one year from that day, he could finally close this chapter of his life. I was under no illusions, however, that it would be an easy year. He couldn't drive home from Hugo. He still had a nerve-wracking year ahead of him, and any violation of the terms of his probation could unravel the whole deal. At the time, both Clancy and I thought that violations would include any sort of traffic infraction, from a rolling stop or failing to signal a lane change. I learned much later that this wasn't true. Our misconception heightened my misgivings. I was worried about the impact of probation on him.

But what options did he have? What options did any of us really have? We had the choice each day to give up, or to go on. And day after day, we all chose to go on. We kept looking forward to each new moment.

Five days later was Father's Day, our first without Pat. Of course, it was on a Sunday and we planned to spend the morning at church. The kids and I were dreading the day but felt we had to go.

In the church auditorium, about two thirds of the way back, there is a massive audio console made out of oak. Pat had made it with help from the boys and installed it himself. Every Sunday, Pat had sat at that console and run the sound system for the services. The kids and I usually sat in the row next to him. Since the accident, without ever discussing it, the kids and I stopped sitting in our usual places, moving further forward to sit near Tracy. It felt like she provided a certain amount of protection for us during the service.

On that first Father's Day without Pat, Sadie and I brought a bouquet of flowers and placed it on the sound booth, then went and sat in our seats near Tracy.

It was a beautiful service. The worship felt to me like I was watching Pat standing before God saying all the words that were coming out of my mouth in song. In addition, a loving friend, Marcy, surprised us at the service to support the kids and me.

After the service, I stood and hugged Tracy and Marcy, feeling uplifted and blessed and ever so slightly less alone. I turned to look behind me at the sound booth, always hoping against reason that I would once again see Pat sitting there with his quirky smile.

I looked up and what I saw broke my heart. There, instead of Pat, stood Jesse. He had crept up to the booth and placed both hands on that oak railing, sobbing. He couldn't tear himself away and I didn't try to make him leave. I just went and stood next to him, my hand on his shoulder, and let him cry until he was ready to go.

Chapter 20

Coffee at Starbucks

It was my 45th birthday. I typed a message on my phone and hit enter, posting this message on Facebook:

"Thank you to all for the birthday wishes! I have clearly seen the absolute goodness of God by the way all of you have loved me and taken care of me for the last 8 months and the special attention this year on my birthday! Many of you have sacrificially given to me and my kids to make our lives easier. I really am grateful for you all! Thank you again!!! Thank you God for blessing me with wonderful friends and family."

I thought about how strange it was that a seemingly silly technology ended up being the avenue through which I could stay in touch with people during such a challenging time of my life. After working, dealing with the kids' schedules, and keeping up with all the details to keep my household running, I had very little energy left over to make individual phone calls, or write individual letters or emails. Facebook, of all things, let me share with all the people who were concerned about me without getting overwhelmed. I'm sure that the founders of Facebook never really anticipated that helping a widow communicate through grief was an aspect of its service that would matter to anyone.

There were a lot of people who wanted to know what was going on, who tried to understand, but who didn't want to intrude or bombard me with questions. I accepted and appreciated the love and support of every single one of them.

There was one woman, however, that I really wanted to talk to. We had never actually met, but I knew about her, and knew that we moved in many of the same circles. Her name was Kathy Ferguson, and she was the wife of a well-known Denver pastor, Rick. Their names had come up many times over the years because their church was focused on the same sort of community-based outreach as our church, L2. Kathy and Rick shared a story similar to Pat's and mine; they'd been childhood sweethearts who married at 19. They'd had three children who were about ten years older than our kids.

In 2002, Rick, Kathy and their 17-year-old son were driving to Missouri for a family reunion. Heading east on I-70, a tire blew out and the car went out of control and rolled. Kathy and the son had minor injuries. Rick was killed. Sadly, their young son was driving at the time of the accident.

The parallels were just eerie. Like our situation, the story had been all over the newspapers and television. Kathy was a widow, left to comfort a son who had been at the wheel and be there for her other two children. I thought about Kathy and her story often, and longed to meet with her. I wanted to hear from another young widow, someone who could help me make sense of my loss. I had so many questions! How do you cope? How did your son who was driving handle things? Was I ever not going to be sad and distracted?

Unfortunately, Kathy no longer lived in Denver. I heard that she had moved out of state and recently remarried. We were, however, Facebook friends, and every time I opened my account, I made a mental note to look for her name to see if she had been online. I hoped for an opportunity to talk in person.

I got my chance in July. I saw on Facebook that Kathy was in Denver briefly and contacted her to see if she might have time to meet with me. She would join me at a Starbucks near my office after work. I was so excited to see her, it was all I could think about all day.

She was waiting for me at the coffee shop when I arrived, and we quickly figured out that we wouldn't have much time. The store was closing in 45 minutes and we would have to leave. I had to get home to my kids and Kathy had another appointment to make. Still, it was probably some of the most important 45 minutes I have ever spent with anyone.

After telling her how much I appreciated her making time to meet with me, I launched immediately into the thought that haunted me. I told her I was beginning to suspect that I would never truly "get over" Pat, that I would miss him forever. I felt that no matter what else happened in my life—remarriage, moving on in houses, jobs or relationships—that I would always, always have a hole in my heart for Pat. I wanted to know if Kathy, who had walked the exact same territory before me, felt that to be true. I'm not sure what I wanted her to say. Did I want her to tell me that I was wrong? That my heart would eventually heal and I would feel whole again and "back to normal?" Or did I want her to reassure me that I was right, that I would never be the same again. If I were honest with myself, part of me was hoping that even in my grief, I would always feel connected to the man I had fallen in love with, the man I had married, no matter what else happened in my life.

Kathy was quick to answer: she told me that even though she had remarried two years before to a dear man she adored—a man who had lost his first wife—she still missed Rick. Sitting there in the coffee shop, Kathy cried with me, explaining that she had mourned intensely for ten months, and was even amazed that I had returned to work as quickly as I did. But, she said, you never truly overcome the grief; you mostly learn to function in spite of it. There's a quote she thought of frequently: If you don't manage grief, grief will manage you. You don't move on, she said, as much as you learn to live with loss.

I found all of this strangely comforting, mostly to hear someone else speak the thoughts that were in my own head, and to reinforce them. I wasn't crazy! I wasn't unusual. So much of what is hard as a new widow is figuring out what your new world will be like without your life partner. Like me, Kathy had been married at a young age and, like me, had never been alone as an adult. After the accidents, all bets were off. Everything we thought was certain was now up in the air and open for change. I wasn't at all sure at that point what my life would look like when everything eventually settled down, but I was so, so grateful to hear that it did not mean I had to let go of my feelings for Pat and my grief at his death. Kathy confirmed for me that I would just have to figure out how to incorporate that loss into whatever life I eventually built.

The Starbucks employees started sweeping around us and moving trash cans, reluctant to interrupt our tear-filled conversation but obviously needing to close. Kathy and I gathered our things and stood to leave, leaning in for one long hug before saying goodbye. She said she would be praying for me, and keeping in touch through Facebook. I thanked her for her time and for her honesty.

I got back into my car and felt a load of tension roll from my shoulders. As hard as my life felt, it was such a relief to know that I wasn't broken. Or, to put it another way, that feeling broken was normal, and maybe even healthy. I would always have Pat with me, even if the cost of keeping him near was grief. Maybe that was a bargain I could accept.

Several days later I woke up after having another rare dream about Pat. I was in a waiting room in some sort of hospital setting. I knew that the doctors had Pat in surgery and were doing some sort of experimental heart transplant after he died for research purposes. I knew he was gone, but felt at peace because I knew his death was serving some higher goal. After they were done, a nurse came to tell me that I could go into the surgery room and say goodbye to Pat. I was so relieved just to be able to see his face one more time.

I saw him lying on the hospital bed, covered with a sheet and his eyes closed. He still looked like the Pat I had known and loved, and I leaned down to kiss him. While I was kissing him, his eyes fluttered open and he came back to life! He lifted his arms to wrap me in a hug and I felt his cheek against mine.

I woke up elated, only momentarily crushed to realize that it had been a dream. I felt Pat had come to visit me, even briefly, and I was thankful.

CHAPTER 21

A NEW SHOCK

It was early August, and summer was in full swing. With Clancy's legal situation at least known, if not resolved, we tried to adjust to a new version of normal with Clancy not driving. He started working part-time for Rachael's father, and picked up odd construction jobs if he could catch a ride with someone. James had a busy baseball season, and Jesse, Sadie and I traded off driving him to practice and games.

Things were more settled, but in quiet moments I still found my mind wandering to thoughts of Pat. There I would be at work, leaning over a patient with tools in my hands wondering about the nature of death and the presence of God—big subjects, I know, while checking a kid's teeth for cavities. But these were my thoughts and I was used to them.

There was one morning at work when I made a mental note to talk to Russ in depth about two different subjects. The first was about how we as humans experience the presence of God. I remembered a song I'd heard on the Christian radio station. The lyrics were about feeling God's presence, and that we could take great comfort in knowing that God is always with us. Intellectually, I wanted to believe that this was true, and I never, not for a moment, doubted that God loved my family and me and was in control of the situation. But feeling God's actual presence near me? As much as I longed for it, it still hadn't happened. I still felt alone and scared a lot of the time. How does God make His presence known to us in physical, tangible ways?

My second question was somewhat related: Is it possible that those in heaven are still fully aware of what is happening here on earth? Was Pat aware of all that we were experiencing in his absence? Was he able to receive joy from watching James throw a baseball or Jesse mowing the church lawn? Did he delight in all that Sadie was learning in school, or take pride in how strong Clancy had been throughout his legal battles? Was it possible that he was able to see me, right then, as I worked with patients, or talked to parents? Did he know how much he was in my thoughts? Was I ever in his?

These were the type of things that filled my mind one afternoon in early August when I got a phone call from Lindsey Bard. I was finishing up with a patient and stepped into the break room to talk to her.

"You have lunch in about an hour, right?" she asked. "We're in your area and wanted to know if we could meet."

"Sorry," I said. "They had to reschedule our lunch hour today because we're so booked. I won't be able to make it."

"That's okay," Lindsey said, "Maybe we'll just stop by your office quickly to say hi."

I figured that because Josh was on the road playing baseball, Lindsey had taken her three children out with her to run errands. It would be great to see her and the kids even for a few minutes. When the receptionist told me I had visitors in the waiting room, I walked out, eager to see them.

I was completely shocked when I saw them. Standing next to Lindsey and the kids was Josh, apparently at home for a rare "off day." I don't know if Lindsey intended to surprise me, or just hadn't mentioned that Josh would be with them. I was so happy to see them all that I found myself choking back tears as I rushed out to hug them all. It felt like the same sort of jolt to my entire body that I'd felt when Josh had called me the morning Pat had died. But this was different. It was a jolt filled with joy. It was a feeling of pure happiness and all I felt was grateful.

When the staff at the office saw how happy it made me to see the Bards, they figured that I needed to be able to go out with them for lunch. Somebody made some quick changes in staffing and suddenly I was free to go. We went to lunch at our favorite spot, Lao Wang Noodle House, and just caught up. After lunch, I hugged each of them goodbye and then went back into work, feeling buoyed and . . . something else. Was this what it felt to be happy? I'd forgotten.

For the rest of the day, this new shocking event was able to replace the ten-month-old event that had consumed every silent moment when my mind was allowed to wander. It wasn't lost on me that Josh had been a part of both of those moments, and I felt such gratitude to him. On that first day, ten months before, he had been willing to break that terrible news to me, and not make Clancy tell me, or have me hear it from a policeman. It was a selfless act, and I'm sure it was as traumatizing and haunting for him as it was for me, which is why it felt fitting that it was his presence that could shock me into joy.

I thought about this later in terms of my question to Russ about feeling the presence of God. It was a theme I would come back to again and again, but I recognized again that day that we are the face of God to each other. God's presence comes to us through them. That day, walking into a dental office waiting room, I truly felt the presence of God in my friends.

Shortly after that, the kids and I attended the wedding for my niece, Molly, to a man named Brian. They'd planned to be married outside near Quinella Pass, up in the mountains west of Denver. Tracy, Sadie, Rachel and I were going to head up earlier than the rest of the family to help set up. We were driving in Tracy's Mini Cooper, stopped at a light in a left hand turn lane on Colfax Avenue, one of the busiest streets in Denver.

A fire truck with sirens blaring and lights flashing came toward us from the opposite direction, weaving in and around the cars that were pulling over haphazardly to make room. Tracy, who was driving, was already stopped and had no place to go. The truck swerved around a group of cars on the other side of the intersection in front of us but in coming back around headed straight toward us. There was nothing we could do but watch as the massive truck barreled closer.

Tracy screamed, "We're going to die!"

I sat in the passenger seat and I watched as the fire truck veered around us at the last possible moment, careening past us on two wheels. My only thought was "Pat, here I come!" My heart raced, I'm sure, but I was surprised that I felt completely unafraid.

That was one benefit of the grief I had endured: I was no longer afraid of death.

We went on up to Quinella Pass and set up for the wedding. It was a lovely, casual affair. Everyone was dressed in shorts and sandals, and the weather cooperated. Clancy came with his cousin Jon to meet us there after the first day of the bow-hunting season. It was fun.

There was a photo booth set up for the guests to have pictures taken using silly props. The kids and I decided we needed a new family photo, so we all donned funny hats and wigs and posed for the camera. I later posted it to Facebook with a message:

This is our family picture of 2011! It was taken at Molly and Brian's wedding, but I think it sums up our life! Crazy and makes noooo sense, but we stand together in support of each

other.

I loved one of the comments I received from Alisa Bard, Josh and Lindsey's sister-in-law. She said, "Awesome!!! I'm pretty sure I hear some chuckles from heaven."

I hoped that it was true. I hoped Pat could see us being silly and happy. I hoped that he knew that we missed him, but were doing our best to move on.

August was also the month of Pat's birthday, what would have been his 46th. He was almost a year older than me but when his birthday rolled around this year, I had caught up to him, something I had never thought would be possible.

We planned to hold a small celebration of Pat's life on his birthday, reserving an event room in our building to host a barbecue for any of the family members or friends who wanted to come. There was no cake. We didn't sing happy birthday. We just gathered family together.

Family gatherings were another unexpected outcome to me after Pat's death. Although both Pat and I came from large families and had frequently been part of large gatherings for both his family and mine, they now took on a renewed importance. It sounds cliché, but death does focus your attention on the relationships that matter.

This had certainly been true for my sisters and me. Both my sisters had moved away from Colorado—Barbara to Oregon and Karla to Texas. Although we remained close, the times we got together were infrequent. This changed after Pat died. We phoned each other much more often, and my sisters made more of an effort to get all of us together.

Barbara's birthday was the day after Pat's, and this year she was celebrating her 50th. She decided against a big party or celebration. Instead, she wanted to spend it with me and Karla. We decided to get together in Austin at Karla's house and then drive to San Antonio to visit the Alamo, a place Barbara had never seen. The day after Pat's birthday, Sadie and I flew into Austin and met Barbara and her husband Doug at Karla and Andy's house. We went out to dinner at a famous barbecue restaurant. We watched the colony of bats, millions strong, which fly at dusk from under a bridge in Austin. We worked together in Karla's glass studio, laughing and working in Austin's 100-degree weather. I felt myself relaxing in the company of people I love, focusing on creating something beautiful just because I could.

I created a small butter dish by combining hundreds of tiny shards of glass of different sizes and shapes. There was no set pattern, just a freeform flow of colors in orange, black, yellow and cobalt blue. I decided it looked a lot like the way my brain felt. I helped Karla load my design into her kiln and watched her set and lock the timer. It took 24 hours for the kiln to heat up and cool down, and I was impatient to see what would come of my design.

Finally it was time to pull it out of the kiln. Karla cracked the lid and lifted my piece, still too hot to touch without gloves, and set it on the counter. The colors had fused and reformed, turning the surface shiny and smooth. It was beautiful. The high heat had transformed it into something lovely I could now use. I hoped, if it represented the state of my mind, that the same thing was happening to me.

Getting to Know
Jesse

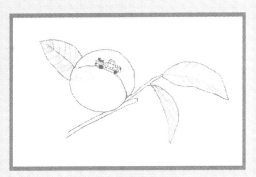

J esse is my third child and my second son. He was born when we were in the process of building our house and were living in a nearby garage. The garage was one large space, and vandals had broken in years before, splashing buckets of bright pink paint on the floors and walls. We set it up the best we could, moving in a bed for me and Pat, and a another bed for Clancy and Sadie. After Jesse was born, we brought him home and he slept in a cradle next to us.

Looking back, it makes sense that Jesse was born in a garage.

In many ways, he shares Pat's mechanical genius. He's meticulous in his work habits, and never seems happier than when he's in a garage, surrounded by his favorite tools, working on a project.

Sometime in that first year after Pat died, Jesse told me a story of one of his last memories of his dad. It was the third week in September, 2010—

bow-hunting season—Pat, Clancy and Jesse's favorite time of the year. They all looked forward to it and prepared for it the rest of the year. With Jesse being in high school, he was unable to miss a week of school and was only able to hunt with them for the weekend.

This year, Pat's friend Collin had accompanied them and had brought a Razor multi-terrain 4-wheeler and my boys brought one of their dirt bikes. They generally hunted on foot but thought these wheels would make things a bit easier. They picked the favorite hunting spot of an old friend, Josh Sheldon. Josh had worked for Pat when he was very young, and heard Pat speak of his passion for bow hunting. Twenty five years later, Josh reconnected with Pat after he, too, had taken up the sport. At Josh's suggestion, they planned to hunt in his spot this year.

To no one's surprise, they ran into Josh as they were setting up camp. They decided to hunt together. Because bow hunting requires such quiet and stealth, they had to split into two groups. That first day, Pat and Collin wanted to hunt a bowl across a valley and up another hill. They'd seen elk there previously. They would hike out and made plans to meet up with the other three later in the day. Josh in his Quad, Clancy on Collin's Razor, and Jesse on his dirt bike would head up the mountain in a different direction.

Jesse knelt near Pat as they sorted out their gear and prepared to take off. Jesse noticed movement in the valley down below.

"What's that?" he asked.

Pat picked up his binoculars and trained them on the movement in the trees beneath them.

"It's a group of people," he said. "Maybe a family. It looks like they are putting up a cross."

"Do you think someone died there?" Jesse asked.

"Don't know," said Pat. "Maybe they're spreading someone's ashes or something."

Both groups left the clearing, heading out for separate areas. Clancy, Josh and Jesse hunted most of the day and no one filled their elk tags. Finally they headed back to the spot where they planned to meet Pat and Collin. After the rendezvous, the group headed back to camp. Pat, Collin, Josh and Clancy led the way on the quad and Razor, with Jesse trailing on the bike. The larger vehicles were much better in that terrain than the dirt bike, so before long everyone was out of sight. Jesse had spent many hours on dirt bikes and was very skilled at maneuvering them, but this one was still a bit big for him. Although he would eventually grow to well over six feet, he was still slight in stature.

Up ahead Jesse noticed a fork in the road. He had no idea which way the others had gone, so as he approached it, he just decided to veer right. It was late afternoon and, as is common in Colorado that time of year, a storm was rolling in. Dark, ominous clouds lurked in the distance. Jesse hung on tightly as he navigated the old mining road. The unused path had washed out creating a v-shape in the center, making it very hard to find a steady spot to ride.

Then the front tire hit a big rock and threw Jesse and the bike off the road onto a steep grassy face. He started walking the bike down the hill when it landed on Jesse's leg, shoving his knee into the hard ground. After he decided that he was okay, Jesse continued to walk the bike on the sheer grass face back onto the road until the bike fell on him again. He tried again. Once again, no luck. He jerked the bike off the ground and threw it on to the rocky road. He was still young, but just like his dad at that age, very strong. He went to upright the bike and started it again when he noticed that the clutch bracket was broken. He was even then very mechanically minded, but all he had on him was his knife. He didn't think that there was anything he could do to fix it, so he decided to sit and wait for thirty minutes to see if the others would turn back and look for him. He wasn't at all sure that he'd picked the correct direction at the fork in the road. If after thirty minutes, if he'd not seen anyone, he would walk back to the fork and go the other way. Jesse had thrown his daypack onto the quad, so he was left without any food, water or even his coat. The temperature was dropping and the black clouds were directly overhead.

Thirty minutes came and went with no sight nor sound of anyone. He stood up to start walking when he heard something. He looked down below and saw the Razor rounding the bend. There was his dad! A wave of relief washed over him as he called out to him. Pat could tell that Jesse had wrecked and first asked him if he was okay. Then he knelt to assess the damaged bike. Pat had some parachute string in his pack that is used as an emergency fire starter, and they used it to tie the cable back together. It worked! They started back to camp when the bike fell again, once again breaking the clutch bracket, but in a different spot this time. Pat, "MacGyver" like, used a rock to press the bracket back together between the lever and the handlebars. It worked again! By now Clancy and Josh and Collin had reappeared and the whole gang was there. This part of the road was so rough that Jesse couldn't ride the dirt bike on the road. Pat tried, then Clancy, then Collin and Josh. None of them could maneuver the bike on that road—a

blow to their egos. Finally with Jesse on the dirt bike, they all surrounded him and pushed it up the final steep hill. Clancy hopped on it and rode it down flatter terrain back to camp and Jesse rode with Josh on the quad.

This story never left Jesse, or the impression he had that his dad was looking after him. When we finally get around to spreading Pat's ashes, Jesse wants to take us back to that hunting spot in the mountains. Maybe there will be some other hunters there who spot us, and will wonder what we are doing.

CHAPTER 22

MESSAGES

It was September and fall was truly upon us. It has always been one of my favorite seasons in Colorado, and this year was no exception. The kids had been back in school for a few weeks and our evenings were once again filled with homework and school-related activities. The days were crisp and cool, and the sunlight glowed on the changing colors of the leaves.

I remembered so clearly what we had been doing a year ago at the same time. We were so excited about moving in to the Wolff house, scheduling how to get the remodel done in stages before the worst of the winter weather set in. Pat was looking forward to hunting season and Denver Bronco football games. Now, eleven months later, that time in my life felt like it happened yesterday, yet at the same time it also seemed like it had happened in another lifetime.

Maybe it had happened in another lifetime. The world I

entered that September was different in every way. I felt like I had made the right decisions in moving forward; there wasn't anything in the past year I would have done differently. I felt more stable and less likely to fall apart at any given moment. I had a much better sense of what the "new normal" was for our family. And although I wasn't happy with the final resolution of Clancy's legal case, it was at least a resolution. We had a much better sense of what we could expect in the future.

And yet, I just couldn't get over the constant feeling that something just wasn't right. I could be sitting at home watching a Bronco game, eating good food and surrounded by people who love me. It could be, overall, a good evening, and suddenly I would be overcome with missing Pat and simultaneously filled with anxiety. Sadie would even notice me becoming uneasy despite not saying a word to anyone. Why does this missing him make me so nervous? I would wonder. This anxiety was completely different from the feeling I got when the kids weren't home and I'd hear sirens. Different from when I was about to speak in front of a crowd. Different from when I noticed a policeman driving behind me. I realized that in all those other moments I knew that the anxious feelings would dissipate when the uncertainty of the unknown was revealed. The kids would come home, unharmed. The speech would be given and over. The police officer would turn off onto another road. But the very certainty of the fact that those moments of deeply missing Pat would never go away gave me a sudden feeling of not being able to live in my skin. The dreaded event had already happened and was certain not to change. Maybe, like my friend Kathy had said, I would never truly "get over" Pat's death. Maybe I would never again feel that things were right. Maybe that, too, would take time. I mostly felt that I wasn't ready for Pat not to be a regular part of my life. I wasn't ready for him to be only a memory to me.

I know how much I craved getting some sort of communication from Pat, as crazy as it sounded. Logically, I knew it wasn't going to happen, but that didn't stop me from texting Pat and staring at my phone, waiting for a divine text message.

It had been almost a year and, other than two wonderful dreams about Pat, I was feeling like I was losing touch with him. I wanted to talk to him about the kids. I wanted to hear from him and know how he was doing. I wished I could have back just one more Sunday afternoon, watching a Bronco game with the whole family, looking through decorating magazines as the boys yelled at the refs and cheered wildly at great plays.

Even a year later, the kids and I still really loved talking about Pat. Ironically, talking about Pat seemed to be the last thing others wanted to do with us. I'm sure people were afraid of upsetting us or making us feel uncomfortable or, even worse, making us cry.

But here's a widow's secret: Sadness was as close and as familiar as any emotion I had. I was sad anyway! I cried often. It takes a long time to grieve a loss like ours, and I learned over that first year that it was very helpful to have someone being willing to sit with me in my sadness, or to be with me when I cried. Most of the time, I wasn't looking for encouragement or advice. I didn't need someone to try to make my situation better, which wasn't possible anyway. What I wanted was for someone to be willing to share it with me. A person's simple presence was healing and comforting, and helped me feel that for that short period of time, he or she was helping me bear the weight of my grief.

I know how hard a task this is to ask someone to do. As a parent, I know how hard it is to watch someone you love dearly feeling so terrible. There is an incredible urge to try to make it better, or to fix the situation somehow. I know now what a gift it is when someone is willing to resist the urge to fix and just sit with someone's sadness.

Strangely, at a time when I was looking for a "sign" of some sort of connection with Pat, I found tremendous comfort in the way all the little children who had known Pat suddenly started to talk about him. Children don't seem to have a social filter about what may or may not be appropriate, and they were happy to talk about him to me or my children without worry or embarrassment. We loved these conversations, and they started to happen with more frequency as we approached the first anniversary of Pat's death.

Josh and Lindsey's kids had a strong connection to "Mr. Pat." Only 4, 7 and 2 when Pat died, they now started talking a lot about how "Mr. Pat" was now in heaven. Their daughter wanted to know if I was now in charge of the family, and had the responsibility for "all those kids." Their son, who loved working with Pat and asked for tools for Christmas and birthday presents, would always meet Pat at the door any time we visited with his tool belt on. But that fall, he seemed so tenderhearted toward me.

The Bard children weren't alone. All that summer, Sadie had worked as a nanny for two little boys, Marshall and Sully, who were the children of one of the dentists in our office. One day, she was driving around with the boys in her car, which uses voice commands to access her phone while she was driving. She needed to talk to her brother and pushed the button on her steering wheel to call him.

"Call Jesse," she said.

The robotic voice of her car's voice system answered, "Calling Dad."

The youngest of the two little boys sitting in her back seat, who was four years old, started laughing.

"You can't call him," he said. "He died! He's in heaven!"

Instead of being embarrassed or worried about Sadie being sad, this little person was willing to talk about what was obvious to everyone. For Sadie, it was a welcomed reminder that, although Pat was gone, his presence in her life was huge and worth talking about.

Several weeks later, I got an email from Pat's niece, Emily, telling me that she'd been thinking about me a lot recently, and wanted to share a story. Emily lived with her husband and two children in Virginia, but they had come to Denver as a family a few weeks before. Their 6-year-old son Corey had been playing video games with James in his room and had seen four fishing poles leaning in the corner. He counted the poles and figured out that with just the three boys in our family, there was one pole too many without Pat. The thought made him sad. After they returned to Virginia and he started back to school, one of their first projects was about fishing. The project reminded him of Pat's unused fishing pole, and it made him too upset to work on the project. He started crying in his classroom, and the teacher called Emily in concern.

When Emily asked Corey what was wrong, he said that he knew they were close to the day that Uncle Pat went to be in heaven. When Emily asked him how he knew that, Corey said he remembered the cool air and that the leaves had been changing. Although he had been off in timing by a few weeks, Emily was astonished that Corey, who had been five when Pat died, recalled the event this way.

A few days later, Emily sent me another text. She'd overheard her kids talking about Pat. Her daughter Aubrey, age 5, said Pat was in heaven building a house on the streets of gold. Her son argued, saying that no, he was fixing a truck. Emily calmly quieted the argument by saying, "I know he is singing. I can hear his voice and see his smile."

I wasn't at all astonished. "Suffer the little children" was the verse that came to mind. I'd come to learn that these little people seemed to have a special connection to Pat that I cherished in those months. I so wanted to hear Pat's voice again, but hearing about him through the voices of other people was the best substitute I could find.

One night, around this same time, I was lying in bed with the lights out, unable to sleep. I kept Pat's cell phone in my bedside table. For a while I had kept paying for his cell phone service in order to keep his answering machine message alive; it was the only recording I had of his voice and I would play it regularly. I had finally let the service lapse a few months earlier, so that night I got out the phone, plugged it in, and was just running through all the settings. I wasn't expecting anything, just liking to hold something that he had held in his hand.

I came across an option for voice memos that I had never seen before. There was one message recorded, so I selected it and hit Play. There in the dark room, I heard Pat's voice, and I felt a jolt of shock and recognition run through my body.

"Here we are today, killing geese, knocking 'em down, left and right. Biggest ones around."

He must have been out goose hunting with the boys and our friend Collin, and they'd been bored, just recording random things on their phones. Not exactly poetry. It wasn't a miraculous voicemail from heaven, as I'd hoped to find, but just this little gift of his voice. And it had been from a time when he seemed happy, carefree and silly.

Maybe this was an early anniversary gift, and the best one I would receive. Pat and I had been married in late September on a date that fell just after elk bow hunting season ended. The year after we were married, the hunting season changed, and from then on, bowhunting season overlapped our anniversary day. Knowing how much Pat loved hunting, I didn't want to deprive him of his favorite activity, and so we usually celebrated our anniversary together either before he left or after he returned from his hunting trip. The last anniversary Pat and I had celebrated the year before was our 24th, and it had been a low-key celebration. Pat was out hunting on the actual day, so I bought and cooked crab legs and ate them with Russ and Tracy. We could not have known it would be our last.

This year would have been our 25th anniversary. I knew the day approached, but didn't make any plans to mark it in any way. A few days before, however, I was scheduled to work in our dentist office in Frisco, a small town up in the mountains of Colorado. The staff usually took the hour drive over together in the same car, and I sat in the back, looking at the mountains, and the colors of the aspen leaves changing. Suddenly, I was ambushed by a memory of a time Pat and I had celebrated our anniversary by driving around in the mountains, looking at the leaves, and visiting many of the mountain homes he had built. I was overwhelmed with both Pat's presence and his absence, and sat in the back of the car, crying. I knew that it was a healthy sort of sadness and let the tears wash through me. My co-workers, who had sat with me crying many times, carried me through that car ride. The conversation that had been on going continued and no one said a word to me. But David the dentist must have seen me crying in the rearview mirror. He reached around his seat and motioned for my hand. He just held my hand. Josh would occasionally do the same thing if I was riding somewhere with him and Lindsey, just reach back and hold my hand. To me it seemed like a conversation without speaking. The gesture said to me that they understood even the everyday things were hard for me and that they recognized it.

On the actual day of the anniversary, I didn't do anything special. It was a Sunday so I went to church, and then had lunch afterwards with Russ and Tracy and the kids. When I got home, there was a message from our building office that I had a delivery, so I walked over to find that Doug and Barbara had sent me yellow roses.

Later, Sadie posted a message to me on Facebook.

I can't tell you how proud I am of your courage and strength getting through this day. You truly handled yourself in a beautiful way. You could have been selfish and made this day about you, but that's not who you are. You always put others before yourself and that is one of the greatest things I admired about you and dad. I can't thank you enough for how you and dad raised us and what Godly role models you were/are to us kids. I know that today seems hard to celebrate and bring joy from, but if it weren't for those 24 years of wonderful marriage with dad, you wouldn't have been able to create our beautiful family. Even if it doesn't seem like celebrating, I am thanking you and dad both, and I celebrate the wonderful life that you have given me as a result of your wonderful marriage and God's grace! I love you to the moon and heaven and back!

After the date of our anniversary passed, I chalked it up to another milestone, another of the holidays or celebrations we would have to live through without Pat for the first time. I didn't realize that I had one more "anniversary" gift waiting for me.

Our friend Collin was selling life insurance at that time and he wisely advised me that I should consider buying some for myself. In the event something happened to me, I didn't want to leave my kids with any debt on the house. I asked Collin to go ahead and write up the paperwork.

As a favor, Collin agreed to bring the papers to my office to sign and he set up his computer in our lunch room so we could work. He turned his computer on and his screensaver was set to a slideshow of the photographs he had saved on his hard drive. I sat there watching the photos, waiting for Collin to finish a document, when suddenly there was a picture of Pat that I had never seen before. Collin had taken it on a bow-hunting trip with Pat, Clancy, and Collin's brother Dallas almost exactly two years before. They were dressed in camo, and Clancy stood right behind Pat with an almost identical expression on his face. Being surprised by Pat's face was such a shock I started crying right there in the office.

"I'm sorry, Collin. You'll have to give me a minute," I told

him. "I just want to keep looking at the photo."

"That's okay," Collin said. "That's what happened to me, too. I didn't know the picture was on my computer and it just randomly came up the other day."

I sat in the dentist office lunchroom for a long time, just soaking up the photo. It was wonderful to find that Pat could still surprise me.

Chapter 23

First Anniversary

My bedroom was still pitch black when I awoke. I looked at the clock on my phone and saw that it was 5:00 am. One year ago at precisely that time, Pat was enjoying his last few moments on earth. It was the one year anniversary of the accident, and I'd been dreading it for days.

I wasn't sure how to handle everyone's expectations about what this day would mean. I knew that I wasn't alone in wanting to mark the day, but I didn't want to be overwhelmed by it. Instead, I decided to control the message and set the focus for the day. I didn't want it to be about sadness. I also didn't want to pretend that everything was fine one year later. I just wanted people to join me in an effort to be faithful, one day at a time. Still sitting in my bed in the dark at 5:14 a.m., I typed a message and posted it on Facebook.

One year ago, right about this time in the morning, Pat got to see Jesus face to face! I'm so happy for him! I'll admit that I have been less happy for us. Here we go, family and friends! Let's tug hard on those boot straps today and show the world that we believe what God said!!! Trust in the Lord with all our heart, mind and soul. In all your ways acknowledge Him and He will make your path straight! Let's just put one foot in front of the other. God will guide us! Whether we eat or drink or what ever we do, do it all for His glory!!! Just like the previous 364 days, let's get up and go for it. Let's act like we believe what we preach. As my friend always says, Bring it!!!! Your A-game!!!

I wouldn't say that even one year later my grief had lessened. Still, I was a bit more hopeful, although "hope" is an inexact word for my state of mind. My feeling was more like "This really sucks but I'm going to wait and see how God uses this."

I also felt like I was on display still, that people were watching my reactions and behaviors, so I wanted to make sure I was sending an honest but helpful message.

The responses started coming in within 30 minutes. Person after person sent me love, prayers, and encouragement.

Many people had mentioned that they wanted to get together on the anniversary of Pat's death, but I knew I wasn't up to hosting a big gathering. I needed another alternative.

I needed softball.

Softball had been a big part of Pat's life and even predated his fascination with hunting. Pat had played softball even before we got married and he had always been a part of a men's softball league. His team, which Clancy later joined, played games nearly every Thursday night. Later, after meeting Collin Myrick, Pat and Clancy started playing on Collin's team. The Thursday night games became a huge part of our family traditions. Sadie, the boys and I would go watch, sitting in the stands talking and eating red, white and blue otter pops.

Pat had died on a Wednesday before the championship game. Most of the players from his team, one of the umpires, and several of the players from the opposing teams came to his service. After Pat's death, Dawn Myrick's brother Paul Cress designed a logo incorporating Pat's jersey number 3 and a paisley, which the team then put on the shoulders of their jerseys the following year.

It seemed appropriate, then, that the anniversary landed on a Thursday, and that Pat's softball team, on which Clancy still played, had a game that night. I figured it was as good a way as any to honor Pat. I invited anyone who wanted to participate to come to the game with my family.

A lot of people showed up, at which Clancy wore Pat's softball uniform and played Pat's position. My kids and I were surrounded by my parents, Pat's parents, Josh and Lindsey, and a lot of other people.

Afterward, everyone gathered at a restaurant called Buffalo Wildwings to celebrate. People had beer and wings and sat around laughing and talking. At the end of the evening, Sadie and I passed out our caramels for everyone. I went home thinking about how different my life was from a year ago.

I didn't know how I'd feel on the first anniversary. I'd expected the year to be hard and it was. We'd had to endure all the "firsts"— the first Thanksgiving and Christmas, the first birthdays without

Pat, the first Mother's and Father's Days—and at the end of all of those I suppose I expected that the worst would be over. Maybe it was, but it was still a challenge.

At the time, I felt like my life was less charged with grief on a daily basis, but mostly I just felt weary. It takes a lot of energy to be sad, and I knew I had to cut myself some slack for the effort it took just to get through it all.

I felt the lack of energy most on behalf of my children. Several days after the anniversary, my kids were all together in the living room. Sadie had a new boyfriend who was visiting and they were all watching a movie. I, however, felt so spent that I found myself in my bedroom, texting Barbara.

"My kids tonight are missing a father and a mother. Tonight I should be sharing in the giddiness of Sadie's new romance! Unable. Too sad! Should be telling Jesse how grateful I am that he drops everything to take Clancy where he wants to go! Showing him how proud I am that he has become the man of the house long before his time!!! Not being there for Clancy who I'm sure desperately needs me to just take him where he wants to go. Not telling James to go to bed or ask about his homework. Does he need lunch money? My poor kids!!! No parent!!!"

Barbara wrote me back. She said that they did have a parent in me. She told me I didn't have to be a perfect parent, just a good-enough one. She told me that there wasn't anyone else on earth more qualified to parent my kids than me. I was good enough.

The image I had in my mind was of a lamp on a lamp stand. The lamp was still lit. It hadn't been blown out, but it felt dimmer. I just didn't have the energy to "light up" anymore. I definitely felt the toll the year had taken on me. My mind didn't feel as sharp. I had a harder time recalling words and memories and important details. It felt like I just couldn't keep everything in my head. I had survived, but it had taken a toll on me mentally, emotionally, physically and spiritually.

I'm sure that from the outside, my life seemed more normal than it was. We had a new dentist named Ashley start at our office at about that time. I was working on a patient with David Strange when Ashley came into the room to watch the procedure. David said, "This is Karyl. She was married to the greatest guy ever and he was killed in a car accident about a year ago. I just want you to know so that there won't be some awkward conversation sometime."

Not put off by David's abrupt introduction, Ashley and I became friends and had several good conversations about times when she had witnessed close friends experience great loss. It had made her more sensitive, more aware of how people are branded and changed by grief. She told me that when she later talked to her mother about my children and me she said she thought we were doing okay.

"Ashley," her mother said, "They're not okay after something like that."

Ashley's mother was right. I wasn't "okay." I probably wouldn't ever be "okay" in the way I had once thought of my life. But what was I, then? I was changed for sure, in some ways more fragile and broken, and in others stronger and resilient. What do you call the thing I had become one year after losing Pat?

This, I later understood, was the central question in becoming a widow. There are so many losses involved. The first level, of course, is the loss of this loved person. I lost Pat and all the roles he played in my life. I lost companionship and support, financial resources and a romantic partner. I lost a co-parent and the person who knew how to fix the water heater. These are the types of losses that most people recognize and expect to come with widowhood. Much of the first year is learning how to cope in the absence of this person. You find someone else to change the oil on the car, you figure out how to make ends meet financially, you get help driving the kids or coaching the baseball team. These are monumental shifts and, if at the end of a year, you've figured out how to operate in the absence of the person you loved on a daily basis, you have accomplished great things.

In fact, the recovery can seem so robust and incredible that many other people expect a widow to be "back to normal" at the one year mark. Before becoming a widow myself, I certainly would have thought the same thing. *It's been a year already. Get over it! Move on!*

I'm learning that this is an unrealistic expectation. No widows I know are "better" at this point. The first year, we swim instead of sink. It's not a beautiful sort of swimming either. We are not perfecting the breaststroke. It's really more of a dog paddle. We simply didn't drown. As a new widow, you need to be patient with yourself and recognize that you will be swimming with more rhythm and strength eventually, but the improvement will come in slow, slow increments. I know this now, several years later, but I wish someone had been able to tell me that on that first anniversary of Pat's death.

I think much of the confusion is that there is another level of loss that many people don't recognize or understand, and this is the loss of your own identity. When Pat died, I not only lost him, but I lost my sense of who I was. I had spent my entire adult life married to this man, and most of my sense of who I was as a parent, a partner, a homeowner, was connected to him. Our ministry through our church was shared, as were many of our friendships. Without Pat, I felt unsure about not only the details of my circumstances, but about my purpose, my career, my vision for my own future. This is an enormous loss, and a nearly invisible one.

And yet, buried within this tearing down of everything you know, there are the seeds for something new, something amazing. A widow has suffered and struggled and survived. But the struggle and the survival does not have to be her destiny. As much as I knew my life felt broken, I also knew that I needed to develop a new vision for myself as an individual. Who did I want to be? What did I want to accomplish? What did I stand for? How could I help? At the end of that first year, I had survived the loss of my husband. The next year was about figuring out my identity, and carving out a new vision for myself.

Around that time, my nephew Sam posted a quote from Elizabeth Kubler Ross (one of the most well-known experts on grief) on my Facebook page:

> *The most beautiful people we have known are those who have known defeat, known suffering, known struggle, known loss, and have found their way out of the depths. These persons have an appreciation, a sensitivity, and an understanding of life that fills them with compassion, gentleness, and a deep loving concern. Beautiful*

people do not just happen.

I had certainly known suffering, struggle and loss and I was, at the beginning of the second year, starting to find my way out of the depths. And what would I find? If compassion, gentleness and beauty awaited me, I would start there.

Chapter 24
The New Year

October 7, 2011 was New Year's Day for me, the day I started the second year of my "new normal" life. It felt like just another Friday. I got up and, still wearing the flannel pants and t-shirt I slept in, rode the elevator in our building up to Russ and Tracy's condo. Russ boiled me two hard-boiled eggs and we sat at their bar stools drinking coffee.

As I stirred more half and half into my coffee cup, Russ brought up the subject I had been carefully avoiding.

"I think you should start thinking about dating again."

"Russ, don't start," I said. "I'm not ready. The kids aren't ready."

This wasn't the first time he had mentioned it, nor the first time I had said I didn't really want to talk about it. But here he was, my friend, my pastor, and Pat's brother, telling me I should think about spending time with someone else. I'd been a widow for a full year. He felt it was time for me to start moving on with my life.

I was pretty frustrated by the suggestion, both that there was something else I needed to address, another item to add to my To Do list when I was still feeling like I was barely keeping up with all of my other relationships and obligations. But even deeper than that, I resented that Pat had left me in this position to have to think about it at all. I hated the idea of being with another man. I didn't want to date. I didn't want to fall in love with anyone. I had already decided who I wanted to marry. I already knew who I wanted to grow old with. It wasn't my fault that that person didn't happen to be alive anymore.

What's more, I felt even more frustrated that Pat and I had come to a particularly sweet time in our marriage. Having just started a business of his own, he had more control over his schedule and was finally about to spend more time with me. The flexibility we'd always wanted had happened, just a few weeks before. Our kids were almost grown. Having had children when we were so young, we'd always planned to have more time together when they were older. We were closer than we'd ever been, just to have it taken away from us. I had a hard time imagining how God could redeem this situation.

On the other hand, I knew that, in theory, it made sense that someday I would marry again. As a young widow with a lot of years left in my life, I wasn't ruling out the option of marrying again. I had loved having a partner, someone to talk to, with whom I could have the sort of mental telepathy that happens from long acquaintance. I longed to have someone to go to a movie with, or to hold my hand on a walk. But nothing in me felt like it was something that could happen so soon.

One day in early November, I was driving to see Lindsey Bard, feeling angry about having to think about the idea of dating. Staring out at a grassy field, it suddenly hit me in a way it hadn't before that it didn't really make any difference whether I was mad or not. Pat still was not coming back, no matter how angry I felt about it. The situation still wouldn't change. I guess I had felt that maybe if I were just angry enough, things would somehow be different.

Something in me shifted there in the car, and I felt a little calmer. I still didn't like the idea of dating, but I was more open to thinking about it.

Later, I told Russ that I was ready to try. We opened a bottle of wine, poured out a couple of glasses and started brainstorming a list of the qualities that I was looking for in a partner. He insisted that I write them down. We joked about the obvious things, like single.

1. Of the same faith
2. Between the ages of 45-55
3. Employed—Stable in his career and financial responsibilities
4. Attractive
5. In good shape

With Russ's help, I signed up for an on-line dating service. I had trouble filling out the profile, so Russ filled in the form for me, adding qualities and characteristics he thought I would like. The initial profiles suggested for me were strange. I kept getting pictures of men, each standing next to a labrador retriever holding fish, which seemed more appropriate if Russ were the one dating them.

I started over, this time really thinking about what I would look for in a future companion. The responses I got back were still very discouraging. It seemed like all of the men within the appropriate age range were either in a gang or living with their mothers. I would scan through the pages of responses, deleting profile after profile. No one seemed even remotely interesting.

Finally I came across an email from someone who seemed to fit the criteria I was looking for. I wrote him back and agreed to meet him for a drink. I went through all the mental preparations for going out on my first date, figuring out what I was going to wear. At the last minute, he called and cancelled. I was both frustrated and very, very relieved.

I kept at it, and eventually made another date with someone else, someone who was intriguing. I agreed to meet him for coffee or a drink and once again started to psych myself up for the date. Sadie had been aware of my explorations in the dating world and was very supportive, but I was nervous about telling the boys.

A few hours before I was ready to leave for my first date, Russ came down to talk to Jesse and James for me. Russ told them that I was about to go meet a man for the first time. Both of the boys cried. Neither of them seemed prepared for the moment and neither of them wanted to talk about it. Russ persisted, trying to get them to discuss the situation.

"I loved your dad," he said. "He was my brother. I know this is painful and hard, but I respect your mom. She deserves this."

The boys stayed silent, crying.

Russ pushed a little further. "You've been kind of denying that your dad is gone," he said, "but this is forcing you to realize that he's not coming back, right?"

Jesse just nodded.

Russ and Tracy took Sadie and the boys out to dinner while I went out and met this man. I picked a place very close to home so that Russ could be there in an instant if I needed him. He was very nice, very polite and respectful, but I had absolutely no interest in spending any more time with him. At one point, he asked if I ever held hands on the first date.

"Since this is only the second first date I've ever had, I don't know, but I'm thinking that the answer is probably 'no.'"

Eventually, I met one other gentleman, also nice, polite and respectful. I still wasn't ready to consider having a romantic relationship with him, or with anyone else. Eventually, I shut down my profile on the online dating site. I knew that it would take a very special circumstance for me to ever become involved with anyone again. It would be someone who understands and can appreciate the love I shared with Pat and be respectful of the life we built together. I was willing to imagine that a person like that is out there somewhere, but at the beginning of that second year without Pat, I knew I hadn't found him yet.

I was grateful to Russ for pushing me to think about the possibility that there is another relationship available for me. I fought against the possibility for myself and for my kids. It was probably a good thing in that it got me to open my mind to another identity, another plan that God might have in store for me.

In the meantime, I was willing to move on in other ways. I decided to focus my creative energies on writing this book with my sister, Barbara. Just before Thanksgiving, Barbara, her husband Doug and daughter Sarah flew out to spend a few days in Colorado. Sarah, a junior in high school, wanted to visit a few colleges in Colorado, so while Doug took her on visits to several campuses in the area, Barbara and I hunkered down and worked on this book.

We sat on the bed in my bedroom and Barbara turned on her tape recorder and her computer. We spent hours talking through the events of that first year. We talked about the accident and those first few days of skin-peeling grief. We talked about Clancy's legal battles and the moves from house to apartment to the townhouse. We talked about Clancy's new girlfriend Rachael and the fact that Sadie had just started dating a new boy. We talked about Jesse trying to work on trucks in the parking garage of our townhouse and James' baseball. We talked about the impact Pat's death had had on so many people, and of the ways people had stepped in to help. We talked about the fact that, as we spoke, our mother was in the other room doing laundry and came in the room occasionally to hang up ironing she had just done.

Finally, Barbara asked me, what had I learned coming to the end of this first year without Pat? What information had I gathered that I would share with another widow following in my footsteps? What would help me move forward into this next new year?

I thought for a minute before I came up with the answer. It was this: I felt my purpose was being redefined, and my work at that point was to figure out what that was. Pat and I had a mission before, but most of it was fulfilled through his activities, especially through the church. He was an active leader at L2, running the sound for church services and events, serving as an Elder, and handling the maintenance for the entire building. In addition, he enjoyed hosting the Habana Men's Nights and various dinners. For all of those, he needed and appreciated my help. Now, with Pat gone, I was looking to redefine the way I served, not as part of a couple but as myself. I wanted to figure it out. This was my New Year's Resolution.

Chapter 25
Winter Stories

SADIE

Sadie had a boyfriend for a brief time who had given her a ski pass as a combination birthday/Christmas present. Shortly after New Years Day—the one on January 1st that everyone other than me celebrates—she and the boyfriend had gone up to Copper Mountain ski resort to go snowboarding. It was a fun day, right up until Sadie fell and broke her wrist. I met them at the emergency room at Lutheran Hospital in Denver.

She had x-rays that confirmed her wrist was broken, and they wrapped her arm from fingertips to her elbow and put her in a treatment room. Her fingers were swelling and turning purple, so she held her hand above her head while we waited to be seen by another doctor.

We had a lot of time to talk. I asked her if she wanted me to see if her boyfriend could come into the emergency room with us, but she said no. I asked if anything was wrong between them. She said there wasn't really anything wrong. He was a really kind, interesting person, but for some reason, she didn't really see herself with him in the long term.

Over the next few weeks, she had to focus on healing her wrist. Luckily, she had finished her practical classes and was taking a more academic course load so she was able to continue with her schoolwork, even with her arm casted. She continued to see her boyfriend, but couldn't escape the feeling that it wasn't the right relationship for her. Josh, who had always joked that he had to approve Sadie's boyfriends, mentioned to her that he had yet to meet this young man. Sadie told him that she wasn't sure it would be necessary. She was thinking about breaking up with him.

Over the course of the next few weeks, she and the boyfriend talked, and eventually decided to break up. The decision, though difficult, felt right to Sadie.

Soon after, Sadie got a phone call from Josh.

"I think I just met your future husband," he said.

JAMES

James is my quiet child. More than anyone in my family, he seems willing to just go with the flow. He's flexible and unflappable, qualities which became very precious to me.

James had never been very verbal about his emotions or how his life had changed after his father's death. He shares mostly through his actions. That winter I started to recognize two things about James. First, he's really funny! With his dry delivery and sly smile, he can have us all laughing in an otherwise tense moment.

Second, I started to recognize that James was very physically and emotionally protective of me. My other three children were rightly focused on growing up and away from me. It was as if the older three children all knew that their main jobs were to develop their own independence at that time, but James knew that soon, it would just be the two of us. He was the one who would notice that I was watching a movie by myself and come up from his bedroom to sit with me on the couch.

One time, we were walking single file along a sidewalk outside of an office building. James walked ahead of me. The pavement was icy and slick, and I noticed that he looked back frequently to make sure I was navigating the slick areas. I began to have a picture of the future I would have with my youngest child, and it comforted me.

When James' birthday rolled around that winter, I sent him a Facebook message:

"You bring laughter into the darkest, most tense times. You were the best surprise of my life!!!"

James wasn't able to get his driver's permit until a few weeks after his 15th birthday; he had to wait for the results of an online written test first. Once it arrived, I took time off work to take him to the DMV, thinking it would be a fun, milestone kind of event. We filled out all the paperwork and, when our number was called, carried everything to the counter. The clerk behind the desk read through everything without even looking up.

"You forgot this section here," she said. "You didn't mark whether or not you wanted to be an organ donor."

James didn't answer right away, and the clerk started to get irritated with him. "You just need to mark yes or no, okay?"

Still no answer. I looked over to see that James was crying, something he rarely did.

"I'm sorry," I said to the clerk. "His dad was killed in a car accident somewhat recently and they donated his corneas."

The clerk softened. "It's okay, honey," she said. "You can cry." She went on to explain that she had lost someone, too, and that person's corneas had been donated as well. She told James she still cried all the time.

She showed James to a computer terminal where he could take his written driver's test, and when he finished we were directed to a different clerk who would grade it. Without looking up, the clerk asked for identification. I didn't say anything, assuming she was asking James. She looked up at me impatiently.

"Oh, you mean me," I said, rummaging through my purse. "I thought you meant James."

"No, we need your i.d. He doesn't have his license yet."

After I handed her my driver's license, she turned to James and said,

"You didn't complete the part about whether or not you want to be an organ donor."

"I'm sorry," I interrupted. "That's why we're so flustered." I explained again about the situation and James started crying again. Twice in one day, when I hadn't seen him cry twice in one year.

The clerk set down her pen and looked James in the eye. "Sweetie, you shouldn't feel bad. Someone donated corneas to my brother and he got to see his son's birthday."

I told James he could make whatever decision he felt comfortable with. He shouldn't feel pressure either way.

James passed the test. He didn't want to drive home, but I drove him to Starbucks for a celebratory drink, and then he drove to school from there. By the time he arrived, he was very happy. He texted Tracy that he had driven to school.

James would be okay.

JESSE

After Pat died, and with Clancy living out of our house, Jesse decided he was now the man of the house. He stepped into that role with intensity and focus. He switched out light fixtures and made repairs around the house. He kept all of our cars running. He remodeled our fireplace, adding a mantel that I'd wanted. I was so grateful, but I worried about it sometimes, afraid that he was, at 17, still too young to take on that kind of responsibility.

On the other hand, I was happy to see that he was building the foundation for his own future. He loved, loved, loved cars. Or to be more specific, he loved trucks. Ford trucks. Nothing but Ford. After Pat died, Jesse inherited Pat's Ford F-150 super-charged pickup, and Jesse took such good care of it. It was a high-performance vehicle, expensive and time-consuming to maintain. Although he wouldn't dream of trading in Pat's truck, he decided he needed something more affordable to drive.

So, he saved up his money and bought another truck. It was a Ford, of course, a 1966 truck. It was a classic, painted in red and white, with red leather interior. The truck was rough, but Jesse systematically rebuilt it, replacing the engine, the transmission, the wheels and much more. I'd see Jesse out in the parking garage of our townhouse, his tools spread out around him, leaning in under the hood of his truck. He worked hard, no question, but this kind of work was also a joy to him. He'd found his calling, or at least a big part of it.

Jesse would be okay.

CLANCY

I'd been so worried about Clancy. His struggles to get through those first eight months of his probation period were exhausting—to him and to everyone else. I've decided that the ability to drive is almost symbolic in our culture, particularly in the west. Especially to someone whose greatest escape is to be able to drive into the wilderness to go camping, or hunting, or fishing. All of that was gone for Clancy, and I was concerned by how disconnected he seemed to feel from his own life and future. Without consistent transportation it was difficult to find a job, take classes, or stay connected with his community. He got tired of asking for rides. He was less able to stay in touch with his girlfriend, Rachael, who was a full-time student in Boulder. He stayed at home a lot. He didn't have much money for food. He lost weight.

He got a white Labrador puppy he named Bella, and he enjoyed focusing his time and energy on her. He lived in the rental house my parents bought, and exchanged remodeling work for rent. He spent time with Rachel when he could.

He counted the days.

Lots of people weighed in on what Clancy should be doing. Lots of people had solutions for him. Mostly, I prayed. I prayed for him to see hope for his future. I prayed that his relationship with Rachael would grow. I prayed that time would pass quickly. I prayed for God's direction in all of this.

February 14, 2012 was a Tuesday, and a work day for me. I

was scheduled to work in the Wheat Ridge office, glad that I would be around co-workers and friends who would love and support me on this second Valentine's Day without Pat. I was happier than I might otherwise have felt, however, because this was the day Clancy's driving restrictions were lifted.

As part of the negotiations, the district attorney had accepted Clancy's word that he would not drive for eight months, and so he had never had to formally surrender his license. Therefore, as of that morning, Clancy could pick up his keys and get behind the steering wheel of his truck. I was just as hopeful that it would allow him to get back to his life quickly. I was thrilled for him to be getting any of his freedom back. As I started working with patients that Valentines Day, my outlook seemed brighter than it had been for a while.

I had only just finished with my first patient when one of the receptionists came back to tell me that someone was there to see me.

What I saw there took my breath away. Clancy came gliding into the treatment area, an ear-to-ear grin on his face. He was holding a huge bouquet of flowers—beautiful purple, white and yellow flowers—and they were for me! The first thing he had done after climbing into his truck that morning was to go buy me flowers.

Of course, I cried, as did everyone else in the office. Clancy was smiling. I set the flowers on the counter and pulled my 6 foot 3 inch tall, skinny son into my arms.

Clancy would be okay.

SADIE

Sadie had gone to Phoenix in mid-February to spend the weekend with Josh and Lindsey, who were there for Josh's spring training. While she was in town, she agreed to a date with a man named Erik, the person Josh thought might be Sadie's future husband. Erik had started his career as a professional baseball player, only to be sidelined after a few short years with an elbow injury. He now worked as a financial planner for other young professional athletes.

He was older than Sadie, and had been married briefly before. Sadie decided that it was worth meeting him.

She called me the next day, more excited than I had heard her in a while. She told me that Erik just might be the one.

"Why Erik?" I asked her.

She told me that she used to say that the most important thing to her in a potential relationship, aside from being likeminded in faith, was that she wanted someone who was funny. Now, she knew from experience that life was serious and messy and sometimes hard, and she wanted to be with someone who could handle that. Erik had already lived through the hard, the messy, and the serious. The events of the past couple of years had opened her mind to people she might not have considered before.

I allowed myself to relax a little bit. My little girl had grown up a lot in the past year or two. She knew what she wanted in her work and in her relationships. She was thoughtful and smart.

Sadie would be okay.

CHAPTER 26

FREEDOM

Clancy had his license back, and had four months left of his probation. The remaining condition left for him to meet was to complete 100 hours of community service. Although he'd tried to complete some of his hours during the previous eight months, his efforts were stymied by the constant turnover of probations officers. Just after he received an assurance from one P.O. for his work site, he would arrive at his next meeting to learn that that officer had been replaced by someone who didn't have records of the previous agreements and who wanted to start the process over.

In addition, there was a lot of confusion over which county had the paperwork to approve his community service. Was it in Lincoln County, in Hugo, Colorado, where the judge had entered his deferred judgment? Was it being transferred to Arvada in Jefferson, County, where he lived? Who was the person who could approve his work?

Finally, Clancy had difficulty finding an approved site that he could reach without being able to drive. He ultimately decided to wait until his driving restriction was lifted, and then to pound out the community service hours in the remaining four months. He set out to get his work site approved so he could get started.

Clancy's attorney thought he could help. As a city council member of Greenwood Village, a small community in the suburbs south of Denver, Gary knew the captain of the nearby South Metro Fire Department and wondered, given Clancy's previous training and his interest in firefighting, if Clancy could get an introduction there. Clancy went to a meeting with Gary and the mayor and the mayor immediately liked Clancy and agreed to try to help him. He sent a letter to the captain of the South Metro Fire Department on Clancy's behalf, explaining the situation and requesting that he consider letting Clancy do his community service there.

The captain got the letter. He wanted to help but, thinking that there wouldn't be enough work for Clancy to do, was leaning towards saying no. However, he decided to run the letter by his training supervisor at the station, a man named Gene Macias, to see what he thought. Gene reviewed the letter. It sounded to him like Clancy hadn't been treated very fairly. He wanted to try to help out. He persuaded the captain to take Clancy on and to allow Gene to oversee his work. He'd find some projects Clancy could work on.

In March, Clancy received word that the South Metro Fire Department was approved as a work site. He drove to south Denver for his first meeting with Gene Macias. Clancy sat down in a chair across from Gene's desk, eager to get his schedule and his assigned duties. Gene opened a folder.

"I've read the file about your probation requirements," Gene said, "but I don't really know that much about you. Why don't you tell me what happened."

Clancy told him that he had been driving his father and a friend named Josh Bard on a hunting trip and had been in an accident.

"Wait," Gene interrupted. "Did you say Josh Bard, the baseball player?"

Gene stared at the file. It turned out that one of Gene's best friends was Josh's brother, Mike Bard, whose baseball coaching business was across the street from the fire station. He had heard the story before from Mike and knew all about it, but hadn't made the connection to Clancy's file.

Gene looked at Clancy, his eyes wet with tears. "I'll do whatever I can to help you, Clancy. When can you start?"

Gene was completely supportive. He assigned various maintenance and construction projects to Clancy, including painting and repairing some of the fencing and equipment. When Clancy finished that, he asked him to dig out a number of Russian olive tree trunks. It was basic, physical work, and Clancy enjoyed it, glad to be working. With every shovelful of dirt, he was digging away at the number of hours required.

Clancy also liked being at the station. Although he wasn't working on firefighting, he enjoyed the environment. The firefighters and staff were kind and supportive, and the hours flew by. He ended up working even more than the required 100 hours, and completed his community service in about six weeks. He had done all he could do to fulfill the terms of his probation, and just had to wait until June when the year would be up. He filled the time by doing some work at our church, and doing construction work with Rachael's father.

Finally, on June 14, 2012, Clancy's probation was over. Although we had heard from Clancy's attorney that it might take some time for the paperwork to be completed, we learned later that the dismissal order was issued right away. All charges were dismissed. Clancy's record was clean, and he could finally move on with his life.

I felt such relief that the huge risk and threat hanging over Clancy was gone. But what exactly did that mean? After being in an ambiguous waiting period for almost two years, what did Clancy want to do?

Freedom is an interesting thing. There is both freedom from and freedom to. Clancy was finally—finally—free from the Colorado legal system and the restrictions it had placed on him. I hoped he was also free from the blame and crippling responsibility that system tried to place on him. He was now free to work or go back to school. He was free to pursue a future with Rachael. He was free to travel. He was free to go hunting. It occurred to me that all of these things, which seemed so normal and so obvious and expected before the accident, were so much more precious after having been denied him.

But was he free from loss? From sadness? Were any of us? Was our attention on moving toward new freedoms and futures, or trying to break free of grief?

Less than two weeks later, our whole family went to Oregon to attend the wedding reception for my niece Katherine. We took our whole family—Sadie and Erik, Clancy and Rachael, Jesse and James, and my parents. My sister Karla and her husband Andy came as well. It was the largest gathering of family we'd attended since Pat's funeral, and it was wonderful to be in the midst of such a supportive family.

After the dinner, Katherine and her father got up for the father/daughter dance. I had known this would happen, and had tried to prepare myself for the reminder that a father/daughter dance was something that Pat had wanted and would never know. I was holding it together pretty well, just trying to breathe, until I saw Sadie sitting across from me, tears running down her cheeks. Then I saw that Clancy, Jesse and James were all crying. It was more than I could take. I got up from the table, trying to make it out of the reception hall before I started sobbing.

Would I always feel this way? In so many ways, our lives had stabilized and calmed in the past eighteen months. But there was still the potential to be ambushed by grief. I wasn't sure if I would ever stop hurting.

Suddenly I felt an arm around my shoulders. Then another. It was Barbara and Karla, who had followed me out of the reception hall, who knew exactly what was happening. I cried and let them hold me. I knew this for certain: the grief was not gone and would probably never disappear. But I knew just as certainly, that there would be people to help me bear it. God would comfort me through the arms of those who loved me.

Several of my kids had to fly back to Denver after the wedding reception to get back to their work, but I stayed on. I celebrated my birthday while I was in Portland. We had dinner at Barbara and Doug's house, and Doug made me homemade ice cream. I was 47 years old. I had now not only caught up to Pat's age, I was now older than he would ever be.

I wondered what the next year would bring.

CHAPTER 27
A LITTLE BIT CRAZY

We moved through the second summer without Pat. Summertime is glorious in Colorado, and I love the long warm days, and the view of the Rocky Mountains from the pool deck at our building. Our lives were once again filled with summer baseball games, barbecues outside, late night swims with the pool and hot tub to ourselves. Looking at our lives from the outside, things started to look a little bit normal. Clancy and Rachael went camping often, taking off on a Friday night and driving up into the mountains. Sadie took some summer on-line classes. She also spent her time working at a local sandwich shop or flying to Phoenix to see Erik. Jesse went through another round of flipping trucks, fixing up an old Ford, selling it, and then buying a new project. He spent long hours in the garage of our building, hunched over an old engine, which we later learned was forbidden in our building. He tried working out on the street, then trailered his projects to my parents' house and worked there. James' baseball was in full swing, both literally and figuratively. He had grown taller, and was becoming even stronger. And I found myself enjoying little pleasures, like a walk around the City Park lake with Adele's music blaring through my headphones, or grilling dinner up on the deck while the boys played in the pool.

But I'll share something I kept a secret for most of the first two years after Pat died: I was more than a bit afraid I was losing my mind. And not just in the "I'm so stressed I can't think straight" way (although I experienced this, too), but in the "I'm thinking thoughts that aren't normal" way. Of all the things I expected about my future life as a widow, this was certainly not one of them. It took me completely by surprise.

The first thing I learned was called "widow's brain." It was as if my brain felt like it was just stretched too thin and decided to check out on me occasionally. Sometimes I would need an instrument at work, one that I used countless times every day for the past 30 years, but I couldn't ask someone to grab it for me because I couldn't remember what it was called. I locked my keys in my car—more times than I could count.

On one occasion, Sadie and I were planning a special dinner to cook at Josh and Lindsey's house and we needed a specialty item that we couldn't find at the local Whole Foods or other chain markets. We went to a specialty store not too far from us, but located in a somewhat dangerous neighborhood. We found what we needed, and when we were leaving the store I started looking for my keys. I couldn't find them. I asked Sadie if I'd given them to her. She said no and walked to the car. I kept digging through my purse and checking my pockets when I noticed that Sadie had gotten in the car.

"Oh nice!" I said, "I left my car unlocked in this neighborhood! Brilliant!"

I got in and started looking around my seat for the keys when it suddenly occurred to me that the car was still running!

Eventually, I learned to acknowledge the fact that my mind was working to catch up with the rest of my life and to cut it some slack. I joked about having "widow's brain" with my family and my friends, and for the most part, people were pretty forgiving of my temporary lapses.

It was this other aspect to my thinking, however, that I didn't share with other people. I found myself having thoughts that were unrealistic or irrational or even a little insane. Even nearly two years after the accident, I would continue to check my voice mail, hoping for a message from Pat. I knew this was an impossibility, but it didn't stop me from expecting that at some point, that message would appear, as crazy as that sounded. And although I knew that Pat's ashes sat in a plastic box in Russ and Tracy's closet, I harbored the thought that God would somehow put Pat's body back together and bring him back to me. After all, wasn't God all-powerful? Surely something could be done!

All the while I was having these ridiculous thoughts, I was also embarrassed by them. It had been nearly two years? Surely I should start feeling sane again soon.

Fortunately, I came across a book that let me know that what I was experiencing was normal, or at least an experience shared with another widow. It was *The Year of Magical Thinking*, by Joan

Didion, and is an account of the year following the sudden death of Didion's husband, John Gregory Dunne, from a heart attack. Her emphasis in the book is less on the specific events of her husband's death, although she covers this as well, and more about her emotional experience of mourning. Reading this book, I was so relieved because Didion put into words much of what I had been thinking and feeling, including my crazy thoughts and my reluctance to move beyond my own grief.

One aspect that Didion covered was the way people responded to her strength in a time of crisis, a strength she did not feel. This resonated with me. I remember people coming up to me, complimenting me on my stoicism, my ability to keep going. They assumed this was sheer personal will and determination on my part. What they didn't understand was that most of the time I was just going through the motions, allowing momentum or motor memory or the sheer force of habit to keep moving me forward. I wasn't actively deciding to be strong. When other people gave me credit for being an amazingly resilient person, I felt confused. I felt I was barely coping and couldn't understand how I was giving this impression to people. I wouldn't be surprised if a lot of widows feel this way for a long time. Didion's book assured me that I wasn't alone.

I was also encouraged to read that I was not the only one who was stunned by memories. Didion wrote about a visit she took to New York City, and while riding on an escalator, felt slayed by the memory of being on an escalator with her husband. She felt that there were places she just couldn't visit during that first year because the memories of him were too intense.

I felt this as well, a strange avoidance to watching Broncos games because I could be surprised by a memory of me snuggled up next to Pat reading a magazine. This was probably less of a problem for me than it might have been for other people because so little of my life was the same as when Pat was alive; I'd moved into a different house, I lived in a different neighborhood. Still, I could look up from the dental chair and see a man standing where Pat would stand when he'd come to take me to lunch. I'd remember his shy quiet smile as others would begin to notice he was there. I'd remember him shaking the hand of the dentist with his incredibly firm grip. I was also drawn to Wolff Street, but couldn't shake the memory of the walk Pat and I took the Monday night before he died, down the street to the nearby Sprouts market, talking about how much we were going to enjoy the neighborhood. We'd even stopped to talk to many people as we passed by their houses and told them we were new to the area but were excited to get to know them.

I finally accepted that I felt reluctant to move on from Pat's death. I didn't really want to "get over" him. I didn't really want to let go. It's not because I wanted to be unhappy, or that I felt guilty about being happy, and I think that this is a misperception that a lot of people have. I figured out that it's about not wanting to lose the connection I had. I didn't want to move on to a life without Pat as my husband. It seemed to me that there was something special about there having been only one man in my life.

I also realized that I don't do change well. I'd led a life of consistency. I'd worked in the same job, lived in the same town, been in love with the same person for several decades. But all of this was forcing me to change. If I didn't want to be alone in the future, I would have to be willing to do something different. I would just have to be able to do it in my own time, in my own way.

I still wasn't ready to consider dating again. Although I know that I would not choose to be alone for the rest of my life, I was not ready to be part of a couple with anyone else just yet. But that didn't mean that there weren't other ways I could work on my future. I'd started to get inklings of an idea about what my own ministry could be. It made sense that it would grow out of the grief I'd felt at Pat's death. What if I could reach out to other widows, especially younger widows like myself?

I continued working with my sister Barbara to write this book, which more and more felt like a part of my future ministry. It seemed like a destiny we were both being called to do. Barbara told me about a time shortly after Pat died that she was walking alone on a beach, her mind wandering as she walked, when she suddenly felt that she was supposed to help me write a book about my experience with grief. When she called and told me about it, it made perfect sense to me. Reading the accounts of other people who had lived through something similar helped me, and I hoped that other people might benefit from hearing my story. I wanted other widows or widowers to feel less alone. I wanted to put words to the desperate moments, the fuzzy thinking, and the small steps out of grief that I'd experienced.

The work had started slowly, taking notes and talking about my experiences. We didn't want to be premature in the writing; we wanted to make sure I had enough distance from Pat's death to have something solid to share. By that second summer, I felt it was finally time to move forward with the book, to shift my attention outward. I took a long weekend and flew out to Portland to stay with Barbara and Doug. Barbara and I sat at her desk for two days, compiling notes and working out a rough draft of the book. We spent a lot of time trying to figure out what it was that I wanted to share.

There was another way in which I wanted to find some positive outcome from the circumstances of Pat's death. I wanted to reduce the likelihood that anyone else would die from a traffic accident at that corner where Pat had died. I continued to believe that if the corner had been adequately marked, the accident might never have happened. I wanted to figure out a way to put up new signs at that corner. It was something I'd thought about off and on, but we didn't want to do anything that could remotely aggravate Clancy's legal position. Now that his probation was finally over and the charges had been dropped, it was time to do something.

I talked to my mom about it. She made calls to the Colorado Department of Transportation to find out what we would be able to do. She learned that it was fairly easy to get the simple blue road signs that said "In Memory of Pat McKendry. Please drive safely." This we would do.

But I also wanted to get directional signage that warned about the dangers of the curve, and to better mark the intersection. Even a stop sign would be nice. My mom finally got through to a woman named Betty who, after hearing about Pat's story, said that the county could order an investigation into the signage for the intersection.

"That would be great," my mom said. "We've heard about

a lot of other accidents that have happened at that corner. But the problem is that the couple who lives at the corner often just helps the driver get the car back on the road and moving on. It's an under-documented problem. There may not be many actual accident reports."

"Well," replied Betty, "we have one. Maybe that's enough."

Chapter 28

The Signs

We'd been preparing for the day for some time. My father had been working to pull together everything we needed and packed it all onto a flatbed trailer. There were sacks of concrete, shovels, and an assortment of other tools. He'd also loaded a barrel filled with water we'd use for mixing concrete as there wouldn't be any water available where we were heading.

On top of everything were the signs. There were two of them, identical. Each was mounted on two 12-foot tall steel posts and held two rectangular panels. The lower panel was larger—about 2' x 4' with a vivid blue surface. In white letters, it read: "In Memory of Patrick McKendry." My father had mounted a smaller sign directly above this. It said, simply, "Reduced Speed Suggested." He had wrapped this smaller sign in striped reflective tape. He wanted—we all wanted—for people to be able to see it.

The kids and I got up early that day. The weather, which

had for days been in the high 70's, had suddenly turned cold. We dressed in warm jeans and jackets and dug out hats and gloves from drawers. I went early to King Soopers grocery store and bought flowers to decorate the signs after erecting them. Clancy and Rachel met us at our house along with Pat's brother Dave and his family, sister Shell, and Russ and Tracy's son Jon. Russ and Tracy came down from their unit and we decided who would ride with whom.

As we climbed into cars, Jon handed me a wrapped package. I pulled off the paper to find that he had printed and framed a beautiful poem he'd written in the year prior to Pat's death, but had come across only recently. When he found it, it reminded him of Pat. Jon said he felt as if it was meant to honor him. When I read it, I agreed.

Orchard
By Jon McKendry

The diligent Farmer lays an axe at the base.
We plead for His mercy.
Such a large, strong beautiful tree.
Surely it deserves more time.

For over the years it bore ripe,
Righteous, real fruit.
Does the Farmer know which tree
He is about to fall?

Surrounded by a forest of
Young, fruit-bearing saplings,
The orchard grows weary as
The final blow fells the giant.

The ground trembles, the crashing
Is heard throughout.
The awkward, awful silence is
Troublesome in the wake.

The roots that once tied the grove together
Dry in the naked sunlight.
The sun begins to beat down
Without the shade.

When it seems that all is lost,
The Farmer nurtures the young grove.
With the extra sun, water and care,
The saplings mature.

The roots that once connected the orchard
Are replaced by new growth.
As more giants rise in the absence,
Their branches reach out.

The trees grow accustomed to
The wind and the sun.
They begin to provide shelter
To other saplings.

The Farmer smiles as his orchard,
Once with one giant,
Now has many.
The process begins anew.

Clancy drove his truck and Rachael rode shotgun. I rode in the back seat with Sadie and James. Jesse rode in Russ's truck. The kids were a bit silly and seemed to be relatively happy, for which I was grateful. My parents, along with Barbara and Doug, drove south from their house in Berthoud, and the entire group gathered at a roadside Wendy's in Limon, Colorado. After a quick lunch of burgers and French fries, we all piled into cars and pick-up trucks and my dad, towing the trailer, led a caravan that traveled south again along a rural county two-lane road.

We drove through a landscape of yellow and brown fields, mostly harvested wheat crops and dried sunflower plants on their stalks. The horizon stretched out underneath a vivid blue sky. A bank of dark clouds loomed up ahead.

I sat in the back seat of Clancy's truck and looked over the landscape. Even though I'd imagined the area over and over in my mind, I'd never been here before. It was both so familiar but at the same time, utterly new.

I looked up ahead at the bank of clouds that hung low over the horizon. A storm was coming.

My dad drove in the front of the line of cars, towing the trailer. Our caravan snaked down the black highway, further and further into the barren countryside. Then we all turned off of the two-lane road onto County Road T. Clancy got quiet. We were almost to the accident site where, two years ago to the day, Pat died.

I hadn't intentionally stayed away from the site. It was a long, long drive from Denver, so not an easy place to visit. Plus, I don't think I'd been ready to see it before.

Now it was time. I, along with everyone else there, just felt a need to see the place, to see if it matched the picture we had built in our minds. We wanted something tangible to connect to, to touch.

But we were also there to honor Pat in the best way I knew how. I felt that the most appropriate memorial I could give my husband was to make it less likely that anyone else would face the same fate he did at that remote intersection. Perhaps Pat would still be with us if the corner where the accident happened had been properly marked, if the road had been properly graded. If, with better signs, we could prevent even one more accident, there would be one more positive outcome of the grief of the past two years.

The road dipped down into a valley before climbing again.

We were surprised to see that the road had been recently paved, and the black chip seal gleamed dark against the dirt. This was completely different. Although I hadn't been out there, my father had driven to the accident site by himself, studying the road, the washed out pavement, the dusty gravel. Seeing that things had changed was a good sign.

When we crested the top of the hill, the accident corner came suddenly into view. I shuddered to think how close it would have come upon Clancy's truck in the cold, pre-dawn darkness. We saw the one sign that had not gone far enough to warn drivers, set far off the side of the road. But it seemed like something was different.

My father slowed down at the head of the line, then stopped in the middle of the road next to the yellow sign. He got out of the car, leaving his car door open, and ran back to our truck. He was yelling and waving his arms.

"They did it!" my father shouted.

We looked closer and saw that now, bolted beneath the curve sign was another: a 30-mile an hour speed limit sign. The kids and I pulled to the front of the line and drove the rest of the way to the corner. A large orange and white striped sign stood behind the corner, and the pavement through the curve appeared to have been regraded. I felt myself well up with tears. They had taken steps to make the road safer. At last. Not soon enough to help Pat. But still, this was something.

Everyone parked their cars and got out. The place was deserted and we all walked up and down the empty roadway, retracing the path through the corner. The clouds closed in and it started to pelt icy bits of snow mixed with sleet. We put on gloves and pulled up the hoods of our coats. The kids and I drove to the spot where Pat had finally landed, where Clancy lay in the dirt with his arm beneath his father's head. Clancy retraced what had happened. He walked me over to the spot where Pat had been lying and said quietly, "this is it." Sadie, Jesse and James huddled closely around me, too. All the other family members started gathering, but kept back and observed.

I picked up a stick and drew a heart in the dirt at the very spot that Pat went from this life to the presence of Jesus. In it, I laid a red rose I had brought with me. Each of the kids placed a coral-colored rose next to mine. Clancy went last and planted his rose upright, its stem in the dirt, the flower reaching up despite the spitting snow. We all stood quietly for a while. After a few minutes, I walked back up the embankment to the road.

"Let's get the signs up," I said.

It took just under two hours to install two signs, one in  each direction. Two crews of people worked, digging holes, leveling posts, mixing concrete. Eventually the signs stood, vivid against the yellow fields. Sadie and I brought out the other bouquets of flowers and a number of us wired the flowers to the signposts. We took photos by the sign, climbed back into the cars, and started the long drive back to Denver.

I sat quietly in the front seat, waiting for the warmth to work its way back into my fingers and toes. I thought about whether the scene had matched my expectations. Amazingly, it had. I had harbored an irrational fear that the vision of the accident that had lived for two years in my mind would now be inaccurate. But it wasn't. As surreal as it had been to be at the spot Pat died, it was also calming and beautiful. The landscape, so desolate and bleak in many ways, was also strangely lovely. It felt perfect in its own way.

So much had happened in the past two years it seemed like a decade had passed. In other ways, it seemed like Pat was still just a breath away. I had spent much of that two year period looking for

many different kinds of signs. I wanted to see signs that Pat was still connected to me from heaven. I wanted to see signs that my life would settle down, that I would be able to come to terms with Pat's death. I wanted a sign that would tell me how God would use all of this in my life, and in the lives of my kids. A road sign wouldn't have been unwelcome, a large blue sign with yellow and black reflective tape that would spell it out for me, make it easy for me to miss dangers ahead, or to prepare for the next part of my journey.

And I realized that there had been some signs along the way. Maybe they weren't as solid and straightforward as the ones we'd sunk in concrete and decorated with flowers that afternoon. But still, there were signs.

I sat in that car, surrounded by my kids, in a caravan of people who knew and loved us, and I knew that God was with me, and he appeared to me in the warmth and care and love of all of those people.

I'd learned that grief is real and lasting, and that it isn't something you can just get over. The grief itself has healing in it, and is a way to cherish the attachment to someone you love. That love doesn't ever go away. You just have to figure out a way to rearrange your life around it.

I knew that I still had a future to live, and that God still had a purpose for me.

A verse came to my mind, Romans 12:2:

And do not be conformed to this world, but be transformed by the renewing of your mind, that you may prove what is good and acceptable and perfect will of God.

In the original language, the word "transformed" was *metamorpho*. We get our word metamorphosis from this. I understand this as a similar process to the transformation of a caterpillar to a butterfly. Is God using all of this to transform me into something He'll use to serve Him differently than I had been before?

Are these struggles and sorrows the necessary steps for me to take in order to have understanding, compassion, gentleness and loving concern for others? For others who have lost loves? Is this His purpose, that I can help others through these unimaginable times? Did He plant the idea in my sister Barbara to help me write this book? The idea excites me!

My favorite verse in all of scripture is Ephesians 2:10:

For we are His workmanship, created in Christ Jesus for good works, which God prepared beforehand, that we should walk in them.

I believe, more now than ever, that God has a divine plan, and that our days are numbered by that plan. That has been the main source of comfort for me since Pat's passing. I have not, however, fully trusted Him for the works that He was preparing for me to do.

I'm not exactly sure where all this is taking me, but for now, I'm willing to keep walking. I'm ready to follow the signs.

Epilogue:

An Open Letter To Pat

April 11, 2014

Hi Honey,

I'm hoping that you can still see me somehow. I hope your connection goes beyond simple curiosity about what we're doing, and that you can see the significance of who we are and how our lives are a crucial part of God's purpose here. I want to think that you are keeping an eye on us. But I still find the need to talk to you sometimes, and to share with you what's been going on.

It's now been over three and a half years since the day you died, and over a year since the day we placed the signs at the site of the accident. A lot has happened since then, a lot of good and happy things, and I wish I could sit and chat with you about it like we used to. I imagine sitting next to you on the bench outside on the porch, overlooking City Park. We could drink a glass of wine, our feet propped up on the coffee table, and we could talk about what's happened. I could tell you about each of the kids. I could tell you what I've been thinking about doing.

Since I can't do that, I will just drink a glass of wine and write this letter to you instead. It will have to do—at least for now.

You would be so proud of the kids, Pat. They've all bravely weathered the past few years, and have worked diligently to build good, meaningful lives for themselves.

The boys are all good. James has gotten so big. He's over six feet tall and towers over me. It's mostly just James and me now. After Jesse graduated from high school, we sold the townhouse and moved into a smaller condominium in the same building. James and I like the snug little space. We have a balcony that looks over the park. We can hear the lions roaring at the zoo. James has such a sweet, funny, light-hearted spirit, which is a joy and a comfort to me. He's very social and has lots of friends. He's started working a part-time job, and he has the tremendous work ethic you always demonstrated. I'm not sure where he'll go to college, but I'm not looking that far ahead yet. I'm enjoying having him at home with me whenever he's here.

Jesse is, as you might expect, totally immersed in cars and trucks. He's earning a degree in auto customization at the local community college, and it won't surprise you to know that he's excelling there. His professors often leave him in charge of the class, he's so confident and skillful at what he does. He's passionate about his work—and his Ford trucks—and has started a part-time business with our friend Jeff brokering cars. He's found a good spot, a good life. It suits him.

And Clancy. Oh, I'm so proud of the way he handled the

long, grueling months after the accident. He could have given up to despair or rage or worse, but he didn't. He hung in there, rolling with the decisions other people were making about his life and trying to make the best of it. He still has his two passions: being an outdoorsman and being a public servant. He's finished his coursework as an EMT and may someday work as a firefighter. In the meantime, he has worked in construction, and at a sporting goods store, advising people on hunting and fishing gear. They were impressed when they learned he knew how to bugle for elk. He told them that you taught him.

He met Rachael, a smart, beautiful, athletic woman who loves our son dearly. I'm not sure how he would have made it through the past few years without her by his side, and I am so, so grateful for her. You won't be surprised that he took on side construction jobs to earn the money to have a ring made, using the same diamond you gave me. They got married last summer, surrounded by all our family and friends. They planned an outdoor wedding, of course, and they both wore cowboy boots. It didn't faze either of them

when it started to sprinkle on the afternoon of the wedding. They simply waited out the rain until the sun came out and said their vows in front of a cascading waterfall. You would have loved it. I missed having you beside me, but I know you would have been happy for all of us. We've often talked about how I always wanted a houseful of girls. And now we have one more. She is so much like a daughter to me, and I am grateful.

And Sadie. Your little daughter got married just a few weeks after her brother. She married Erik, the smart, committed man Josh introduced her to. It's almost magical how good he is with people, how outgoing and social he is. He and Sadie make a great team in how they complement each other. They have been very intentional about their life together, figuring how to support both of their passions for work, Sadie in her culinary arts and Erik in his work with young athletes. They are planning a life in Arizona.

As excited as we all were for their marriage, we were a little bit nervous about their wedding. It would be so obvious to us that you wouldn't be there to walk your little girl down the aisle, or to have the father/daughter dance with your own Cinderella. After all, it was on your bucket list the night before you died.

But the day of their wedding was a bit of a miracle in itself. It was held at our church. The auditorium was simply decorated, and we set up the reception in the downstairs hall. We worked for months on the decorations and flower arrangements and menus. It was beautiful and candle-lit and elegant.

Russ presided over the ceremony, of course, and stood at the front of the church waiting with Erik for Sadie to walk down the aisle. We all looked to the back of the church to see your darling girl standing in a strapless white dress. She was smiling. Beaming! She wasn't nervous or scared or sad at all.

Her brothers walked her down the aisle. She started out with James, who passed her on to Jesse, who then escorted her to Clancy. Clancy walked the remaining steps down to the altar to meet Erik. Everyone in the church was crying, thinking about you, thinking about how much you would have wanted to be there.

But here's the strange thing. Sadie told me later that she felt nothing but peace and joy. It was like a little miracle to her, that a day that could have carried sadness was bright and beautiful. She knew in her heart that everything was actually okay. You were fine. She was fine. And she was so happy to be getting married. It showed on her face.

After the wedding ceremony and the dinner, there was dancing. My dad figured out how to set up a dance floor on the terrace in front of the church, and had lit it with overhead twinkle lights. Some of my friends from work provided the music, and she and Erik walked out onto the dance floor for their first dance. She didn't get to do her father/daughter dance, but she and Erik had worked on a beautifully choreographed dance together, and performed it flawlessly. Sadie had even bought a dress that would accommodate the complicated tricks they would perform.

The dress was special in another way. She needed to acknowledge your importance in that moment, but she didn't want the moment to be sad or to take away from her time with Erik. So she cut a heart out of that red striped polo shirt you used to wear all the time, and had my mom sew it onto the back of her wedding gown. She also put a framed photo of the two of you dancing near the dance floor. You were there with us that night.

I'm looking forward to the day in, say, 70 years or so, that you get to meet both Rachael and Erik. You'll love them as I do, and they will both finally understand how much like you Clancy and Sadie are.

And me? I still miss you, of course, but I've come to realize that no matter what, your spirit and memory come with me. I don't expect that ever to change, regardless of where my life leads me. But after nearly four years, I think I've started to move on to the next part of my life, the part that makes sense for now. With Sadie living out of state, our dreams of running a cafe have shifted. We're now figuring out other ways we can produce and sell caramels and whatever other delicious ideas we come up with.

But I've figured out another ministry as well, one you indirectly led me to. Over the past several years I've recognized a need for more support for widows, especially young ones. Widowhood is so isolating, and so misunderstood. I've met a number of other widows who agree with me, and we're working together to redefine what widowhood looks like. I'm starting a non-profit organization called the Paisley Project, inspired by that pink paisley shirt you loved so much. We want to open up widowhood to new light and air. We want to reduce the isolation, and make room for grief and joy and rebuilding. We want to help other people find the most meaningful, most helpful ways to support widows. We haven't figured it all out yet, but Pat, I'm as excited by this as I have been by anything since the day you died. I finally have an idea of what God put me on this earth to do. Not surprisingly, you were a part of that as well.

You are always with me, honey, your dimpled grin and icy-blue eyes. I imagine your arms around me, holding me, supporting me. You'd be proud of me, I know.

Just remember. I love you to the moon and back.

Heart, moon, swirly thing.

Love always,

Karyl

JOIN THE PAISLEY PROJECT TEAM!

At the Paisley Project, we help young widows not just to survive, but to thrive. We support them as they move from the point of Loss, to the point of new Identity, and on to a new Vision for the future, a pathway we've shortened to L.I.V.

The Paisley Project name was inspired by a fabulous pink paisley shirt that my husband Pat loved. I was intrigued to learn that the paisley design, called a *boteh*, was inspired by a cypress tree, long associated with both mourning and eternity.

Paisley Project is committed to connecting one widow to another, providing practical tools for surviving the initial 12-18 months, but also offering education and resources for the supporters of widows who want to help but don't know how. We are excited about helping young-minded widows reinvent their lives. We believe this is a process requires a community of committed creative supporters behind it. The Paisley Project team is just that.

If you are a widow, or would like to provide support to widows, we invite you to participate in the Paisley Project community. Please visit our website at **www.PaisleyProject.org** to find resources, information, and an online community. You can donate to Paisley Project to support our ongoing activities.

You can also order additional copies of *Lovely Tragic Miracle* from our website.

Join us!

Karyl McKendry, Executive Director
The Paisley Project

34214499R00161

Made in the USA
Charleston, SC
04 October 2014